ULTIMATE

THE

CROCKP

COOKBOOK FOR BEGINN

FOR EVERYDAY SLOW COOKING

Table of Contents

INTRODUCTION

Discover the art of slow cooking with the versatile and convenient Crockpot. This special ceramic or terracotta pot, equipped with a heating element, revolutionizes meal preparation, allowing you to create delicious dishes with minimal effort and maximum flavor. Let's delve into the world of slow cooking and unlock its many benefits, from economical meal options to effortless culinary mastery.

Economical:

Embrace the cost-saving potential of slow cooking with the Crockpot. By harnessing low temperatures and extended cooking times, you can transform budget-friendly cuts of meat into tender, flavorful meals. Alternatively, opt for hearty vegetable-centric dishes that promote health and wellness without breaking the bank.

No Need for Excess Oil and Fat:

Bid farewell to unnecessary oils and fats when using the Crockpot for your culinary creations. Thanks to its unique design, food doesn't stick to the pot's surface as long as it maintains the right level of moisture. Experience the full depth of flavor without the guilt of excessive fats, as slow cooking allows rich flavors to develop naturally over time.

Unsupervised Cooking:

Experience the freedom of unattended cooking with the Crockpot. Simply set it and forget it, knowing that you'll return to a piping hot stew or soup ready to nourish and delight. Whether you're off to work or drifting off to sleep, the Crockpot ensures that delicious meals are always within reach, making every day a culinary delight.

No Special Kitchen Skills Required:

Say goodbye to kitchen anxiety and hello to culinary confidence with the Crockpot. With its simple operation and effortless cooking process, anyone can become a master chef. Just add your ingredients, set the timer, and let the Crockpot work its magic, transforming basic ingredients into extraordinary meals with ease.

Save Time and Effort:

Reclaim your time and energy with the Crockpot's efficient cooking capabilities. With the Crockpot, cooking becomes a pleasure rather than a chore, allowing you to savor every moment in the kitchen.

Key Tips for Successful Slow Cooking:

Choose the right meat: Opt for cuts that thrive under slow cooking conditions, such as lamb shanks, beef chuck roast, or pork shoulder, to ensure optimal flavor and tenderness.

Caramelize the Meat:

Enhance the depth of flavor by browning your meat before slow cooking, ensuring a rich and savory result.

Avoid Overfilling the Pot:

Maintain optimal cooking conditions by not overfilling the Crockpot, allowing ingredients to cook evenly and thoroughly.

Thaw Frozen Ingredients:

Ensure safe and delicious results by thawing frozen ingredients before adding them to the Crockpot, preventing uneven cooking and potential food safety issues.

CHAPTER 1
APPETIZER RECIPES

Sausage Dip

Time: 6 hrs 15 mins   **Servings: 8**

Ingredients:
1 can diced tomatoes
1 pound fresh pork sausage
2 poblano peppers, chopped
1 cup cream cheese
1 pound spicy pork sausages

Directions:
1. Mix all the ingredients in the crock pot.
2. Cook for a total of six hours on low.
3. Serve hot or cold.

Spiced Buffalo Wings

Time: 8 hrs 15 mins   **Servings: 8**

Ingredients:
4 pounds chicken wings
1 cup BBQ sauce
1 teaspoon hot sauce
1 teaspoon onion powder
1/2 teaspoon cumin powder
1/2 teaspoon cinnamon powder
1 teaspoon salt
1/4 cup butter, melted
1 tablespoon Worcestershire sauce
1 teaspoon dried oregano
1 teaspoon dried basil
1 teaspoon garlic powder

Directions:
1. Put all the ingredients into a slow cooker and mix well.
2. Continue to stir until the wings are completely coated.
3. Cook for a total of eight hours in a low setting.
4. Serve either hot or cold.

Tropical Meatballs

Time: 7 hrs 30 mins   **Servings: 20**

Ingredients:
2 poblano peppers, chopped
2 tablespoons soy sauce
1 tablespoon lemon juice
1 pound ground beef
4 garlic clove, minced
1 egg
1 can pineapple chunks and juice
1/4 cup brown sugar
2 tablespoons cornstarch
2 pounds ground pork
1 teaspoon dried basil
1/4 cup breadcrumbs
Salt and pepper

Directions:
1. In a slow cooker, combine the poblano peppers, pineapple and juice, soy sauce, cornstarch, brown sugar, and lemon juice.
2. In a bowl, combine the breadcrumbs, garlic, egg, basil, and ground beef. Mix everything together after adding salt and pepper to taste.
3. Make small meatballs and put them in the sauce.
4. Cover and cook on low for seven hours.
5. Serve warm.

Glazed Peanuts

Time: 2 hrs 15 mins   **Servings: 8**

Ingredients:
2 pounds raw, whole peanuts
1/4 cup brown sugar
1/2 teaspoon garlic powder
2 tablespoons salt
1 tablespoon Cajun seasoning
1/2 teaspoon red pepper flakes
1/4 cup coconut oil

Directions:
1. Put all the ingredients in your slow cooker.
2. Cover and cook on high for two hours.
3. Serve hot or cold.

Ham and Swiss Cheese Dip

Time: 4 hrs 15 mins   Servings: 6

Ingredients:
1 cup cream cheese
1/2 teaspoon chili powder
1 can condensed onion soup
1 pound ham, diced
2 cups grated Swiss cheese
1 can condensed cream of mushroom soup

Directions:
1. Place all ingredients in a slow cooker.
2. Cook on low for 4 hours.
3. Serve the ham and Swiss dip warm.

Spanish Chorizo Dip

Time: 6 hrs 15 mins   Servings: 8

Ingredients:
2 cups grated Cheddar cheese
8 chorizo links, diced
1 chili pepper, chopped
1 cup cream cheese
1 can diced tomatoes
1/4 cup white wine

Directions:
1. Place all ingredients in your slow cooker.
2. Cook on low for 6 hours.
3. Serve the dip hot or cold.

Mexican Dip

Time: 4 hrs 15 mins   Servings: 10

Ingredients:
2 cups grated Cheddar cheese
1 can black beans, drained
2 poblano peppers, chopped
1/2 teaspoon chili powder
1 can diced tomatoes
Salt and pepper
2 pounds ground beef

Directions:
1. Combine all ingredients in a slow cooker.
2. Sprinkle with salt and pepper to taste.
3. Cook for 4 hours on high.
4. Serve warm.

Asian Marinated Mushrooms

Time: 8 hrs 15 mins   Servings: 8

Ingredients:
1/4 cup rice vinegar
1 cup water
2 pounds mushrooms
1/2 cup brown sugar
1 cup soy sauce
1/2 teaspoon chili powder

Directions:
1. Place all ingredients in your slow cooker.
2. Cover the crock pot and cook for 8 hours on low.
3. Set aside to cool in the pot before serving.

Nacho Sauce

Time: 6 hrs 15 mins   **Servings: 12**

Ingredients:
4 garlic cloves, minced
2 tablespoons Mexican seasoning
1 teaspoon chili powder
2 pounds ground beef
2 shallots, chopped
1 can sweet corn, drained
2 cups grated cheddar cheese
1 can diced tomatoes

Directions:
1. Put all the ingredients in the slow cooker.
2. Cook for 6 hours on low.
3. Serve warm.

Five-Spice Chicken Wings

Time: 7 hrs 15 mins   **Servings: 8**

Ingredients:
1/2 cup plum sauce
1/2 cup BBQ sauce
2 tablespoons butter
1 tablespoon five-spice powder
1 teaspoon salt
1/2 teaspoon chili powder
4 pounds chicken wings

Directions:
1. Combine the butter, plum sauce, five-spice, salt, BBQ sauce, and chili powder in a crock pot.
2. Mix well until, then add chicken wings and coat completely.
3. Cover and cook the dish for 7 hours on low.
4. Serve either hot or cold.

Queso Verde Dip

Time: 4 hrs 15 mins   **Servings: 12**

Ingredients:
1 pound ground chicken
2 shallots, chopped
2 tablespoons olive oil
2 cups salsa verde
1 cup cream cheese
2 cups grated cheddar cheese
2 poblano peppers, chopped
1 tablespoon Worcestershire sauce
4 garlic cloves, minced
1/4 cup chopped cilantro
Salt and pepper to taste

Directions:
1. Put all the ingredients in the slow cooker.
2. Add salt and pepper to taste and cook for 4 hours on low.
3. Serve warm.

Party Mix

Time: 1 hr 45 mins   **Servings: 20**

Ingredients:
4 cups crunchy cereals
2 cups mixed nuts
1 cup mixed seeds
1/2 cup butter, melted
2 tablespoons Worcestershire sauce
1 teaspoon hot sauce
1 teaspoon salt
1/2 teaspoon cumin powder

Directions:
1. Put all the ingredients in the slow cooker and mix well, until cereal is evenly coated.
2. Cook for 90 mins on high.
3. Serve the mixture warm or at room temperature.

Caramelized Onion Dip

Time: 4 hrs 30 mins   **Servings: 12**

Ingredients:

4 red onions, sliced
1 tablespoon canola oil
1 teaspoon dried thyme
2 garlic cloves, chopped
2 cups grated Swiss cheese

2 tablespoons butter
1 cup beef stock
1/2 cup white wine
Salt and pepper
1 tablespoon cornstarch

Directions:

1. In a pan, heat the butter and oil over medium heat. Add onions and cook until they start to caramelize.
2. Place the onions and the rest of the ingredients in your slow cooker.
3. Add salt and pepper, then cook for 4 hours on low heat.
4. Serve the warm dip with veggie sticks or your preferred crunchy foods.

Bourbon-Glazed Sausages

Time: 4 hrs 15 mins   **Servings: 10**

Ingredients:

2 tablespoons Bourbon
3 pounds small sausage links
1/4 cup maple syrup
1/2 cup apricot preserves

Directions:

1. Put all the ingredients in the slow cooker.
2. Cover and cook for 4 hours on low,
3. Serve the glazed sausages hot or cold, preferably with cocktail sticks.

Sweet Corn Crab Dip

Time: 2 hrs 15 mins   **Servings: 20**

Ingredients:

1 cup canned sweet corn, drained
1 teaspoon Worcestershire sauce
2 garlic cloves, chopped
1 cup sour cream
1 teaspoon hot sauce
2 tablespoons butter
2 poblano peppers, chopped
1 can crab meat, drained
2 red bell peppers, cored and diced
1 cup grated cheddar cheese

Directions:

1. Put all the ingredients in the slow cooker and stir.
2. Cover and cook for 2 hours on low.
3. Serve the dip hot or cold.

Rosemary Potatoes

Time: 2 hrs 15 mins   **Servings: 8**

Ingredients:

4 pounds small new potatoes
1 rosemary sprig, chopped
1 shallot, sliced
2 garlic cloves, chopped
1 teaspoon smoked paprika
1 teaspoon salt
1/4 teaspoon ground black pepper
1/4 cup chicken stock

Directions:

1. Put all the ingredients in the slow cooker.
2. Cover and cook for 2 hours on high.
3. Serve the potatoes hot or cold.

Blue Cheese Chicken Wings

Time: 7 hrs 15 mins   **Servings: 8**

Ingredients:
1 cup sour cream
1 thyme sprig
1/2 cup buffalo sauce
2 oz. blue cheese, crumbled
4 pounds chicken wings
1 tablespoon Worcestershire sauce
1 tablespoon tomato paste
2 tablespoons apple cider vinegar
1/2 cup spicy tomato sauce

Directions:
1. Put the tomato sauce, buffalo sauce, Worcestershire sauce, vinegar, blue cheese, sour cream, and thyme in a slow cooker.
2. Add the chicken wings and coat completely with sauce.
3. Cook for 7 hours on low.
4. Serve warm.

Creamy Spinach Dip

Time: 2 hrs 15 mins   **Servings: 30**

Ingredients:
1 can crab meat, drained
1 cup grated Parmesan
1 cup sour cream
1 tablespoon sherry vinegar
2 jalapeno peppers, chopped
1 pound fresh spinach, chopped
2 shallots, chopped
1/2 cup whole milk
1 cup cream cheese
2 garlic cloves, chopped
1 cup grated cheddar cheese

Directions:
1. Put all the ingredients in the slow cooker.
2. Cover and cook for 2 hours on high.
3. Serve the spinach dip warm with vegetable stick or your preferred salty snacks.

Cheesy Bacon Dip

Time: 4 hrs 15 mins   **Servings: 20**

Ingredients:
10 bacon slices, chopped
Salt and pepper
1/2 cup whole milk
1 cup grated Gruyere
1 teaspoon Dijon mustard
1 cup cream cheese
1 sweet onions, chopped
1 teaspoon Worcestershire sauce

Directions:
1. Put all the ingredients in the slow cooker.
2. Add salt and pepper to taste and cover.
3. Cook for 4 hours on low.
4. Serve the dip hot or cold with vegetable sticks, crackers, or other salty snacks.

Artichoke Dip

Time: 6 hrs 15 mins   **Servings: 20**

Ingredients:
2 oz. blue cheese, crumbled
2 garlic cloves, chopped
2 sweet onions, chopped
1 red chili, chopped
1 cup cream cheese
1 cup heavy cream
2 tablespoons chopped cilantro
1 jar artichoke hearts, drained and chopped

Directions:
1. Add the garlic, heavy cream, chili, artichoke hearts, onions, cream cheese, and blue cheese in the slow cooker and mix.
2. Cook for 6 hours on low.
3. When done, add the cilantro and serve warm.

Chili Chicken Wings

Time: 7hrs 15 mins   **Servings: 8**

Ingredients:

4 pounds chicken wings
1 teaspoon garlic powder
2 tablespoons balsamic vinegar
1 tablespoon Dijon mustard
1 teaspoon Worcestershire sauce
1/4 cup maple syrup
1 teaspoon chili powder
1 teaspoon salt
1/2 cup tomato sauce

Directions:

1. Mix all ingredients in the slow cooker.
2. Stir until chicken wings are completely coated; cook for 7 hours on low.
3. Serve the chicken wings hot or cold.

Chipotle BBQ Meatballs

Time: 7 hrs 30 mins   **Servings: 10**

Ingredients:

3 pounds ground pork
1 bay leaf
2 shallots, chopped
2 chipotle peppers, chopped
Salt and pepper
2 garlic cloves, minced
2 cups BBQ sauce
1/4 cup cranberry sauce

Directions:

1. Add the garlic, ground pork, chipotle peppers, shallots, and salt and pepper in a bowl and mix.
2. Mix the cranberry sauce, BBQ sauce, and bay leaf in your slow cooker.
3. Form small meatballs and place them in the sauce.
4. Cover the pot and cook on low for 7 hours.
5. Serve the meatballs hot or cold with cocktail skewers or toothpicks.

Chipotle BBQ Sausage Bites

Time: 2 hrs 15 mins   **Servings: 10**

Ingredients:

Salt and pepper
2 chipotle peppers in adobo sauce
1 cup BBQ sauce
1 tablespoon tomato paste
3 pounds small smoked sausages
1/4 cup white wine

Directions:

1. Put all the ingredients in your slow cooker.
2. Add salt and pepper to taste, then cover.
3. Cook for 2 hours on high.
4. Serve the BBQ sausage bites hot or cold.

Cheesy Chicken Bites

Time: 6 hrs 30 mins   **Servings: 10**

Ingredients:

2 roasted red bell peppers
1/4 cup all-purpose flour
Salt and pepper
1 cup cream cheese
1 cup shredded mozzarella cheese
1/4 teaspoon chili powder
4 chicken breasts, cut into bite-size cubes

Directions:

1. Place the bell peppers, cream cheese, salt, chili powder, and pepper in a blender and blend until smooth.
2. Put the mixture in your slow cooker and add the remaining ingredients.
3. Cook for 6 hours on low.
4. Serve the chicken bites hot or cold.

Pork & Ham Dip

Time: 6 hrs 15 mins   Servings: 20

Ingredients:
1/2 cup cranberry sauce   2 cups diced ham
1 cup tomato sauce   1/2 cup chili sauce
1 shallot, chopped   2 garlic cloves, chopped
1 pound ground pork   1 teaspoon Dijon mustard
Salt and pepper

Directions:
1. Heat a pan over medium heat and add the ground pork. Cook for 5 minutes, stirring often.
2. Place the ground pork in a slow cooker and add the remaining ingredients.
3. Add salt and pepper to taste and cook for 6 hours on low.
4. Serve the pork ham dip hot or cold.

Cranberry Sauce Meatballs

Time: 7 hrs 30 mins   Servings: 12

Ingredients:
1 egg   3 pounds ground pork
1 thyme sprig   1 pound ground turkey
1 shallot, chopped   1/2 cup breadcrumbs
1 cup BBQ sauce   1/2 teaspoon ground cloves
2 cups cranberry sauce   1 teaspoon hot sauce
Salt and pepper

Directions:
1. Combine the turkey, ground pork, egg, breadcrumbs, salt, ground cloves, shallot, and pepper and mix well.
2. Combine the BBQ sauce, cranberry sauce, hot sauce, and thyme sprig in your slow cooker.
3. Form small meatballs and place them in the sauce.
4. Cook for 7 hours on low.
5. Serve the meatballs hot or cold.

Honey Chicken Drumsticks

Time: 7 hrs 15 mins   Servings: 8

Ingredients:
1 teaspoon rice vinegar
1/2 teaspoon dried Thai basil
1/4 cup soy sauce
2 tablespoons tomato paste
1/4 cup honey
3 pounds chicken drumsticks
1/2 teaspoon sesame oil

Directions:
1. Put all the ingredients in your slow cooker and mix until drumsticks are completely coated.
2. Cover and cook for 7 hours on low.
3. Serve the chicken drumsticks hot or cold.

Cheeseburger Dip

Time: 6 hrs 15 mins   Servings: 20

Ingredients:
2 pounds ground beef   1 tablespoon canola oil
2 sweet onions, chopped   4 garlic cloves, chopped
1/2 cup tomato sauce   1 tablespoon Dijon mustard
2 tablespoons pickle relish   1 cup grated cheddar
1 cup shredded American cheese

Directions:
1. Heat the canola oil in a pan and add the ground beef. Sauté for 5 minutes then place in your slow cooker.
2. Add the remaining ingredients and cover.
3. Cook for 6 hours on low.
4. Serve warm.

Bacon Crab Dip

Time: 2 hrs 15 mins   **Servings: 20**

Ingredients:
1 teaspoon Dijon mustard
1 teaspoon hot sauce
1 cup cream cheese
1/2 cup grated Parmesan cheese
1 pound bacon, diced
1 teaspoon Worcestershire sauce
1 can crab meat, drained and shredded

Directions:
1. Place a pan over medium heat and add the bacon. Sauté for 5 minutes until fat starts draining out.
2. Place the bacon in a slow cooker.
3. Add the remaining ingredients and cook for 2 hours on high.
4. Serve the dip hot or cold.

Curried Chicken Wings

Time: 7 hrs 15 mins   **Servings: 10**

Ingredients:
Salt and pepper to taste
1 cup tomato sauce
1/2 cup coconut milk
4 pounds chicken wings
2 shallots, chopped
1/4 cup red curry paste
1/2 teaspoon dried basil

Directions:
1. Put all the ingredients in a slow cooker and stir well until chicken is completely coated.
2. Add salt and pepper and cook for 7 hours on low.
3. Serve the chicken wings hot or cold.

Wild Mushroom Dip

Time: 4 hrs 15 mins   **Servings: 20**

Ingredients:
1 cup white wine   1 cup cream cheese
1 cup heavy cream   1/2 cup grated Parmesan
1 teaspoon dried tarragon   1/2 teaspoon dried oregano
1/2 teaspoon ground black pepper
Salt and pepper
1-pound wild mushrooms, chopped
1 can condensed cream of mushroom soup

Directions:
1. Put all the ingredients in your slow cooker.
2. Add salt and pepper and cook for 4 hours on low.
3. Serve the dip hot or cold.

Mediterranean Dip

Time: 6 hrs 15 mins   **Servings: 20**

Ingredients:
2 tablespoons canola oil
2 shallots, chopped
2 garlic cloves, chopped
1/4 cup white wine
1 pound ground beef
1/2 cup tomato sauce
4 ripe tomatoes, peeled and diced
1/2 cup black olives, pitted and chopped
1/2 cup Kalamata olives, pitted and chopped
1/2 teaspoon dried oregano
1 teaspoon dried basil
Salt and pepper

Directions:
1. Place a pan over medium heat and add the beef. Cook for 5 minutes then add the shallots and garlic and cook for another 5 minutes.
2. Transfer the mixture to your slow cooker and add the remaining ingredients.
3. Add salt and pepper to taste and cook for 6 hours on low.
4. Serve the dip hot or cold.

Bacon New Potatoes

Time: 3 hrs 15 mins　　　**Servings: 6**

Ingredients:
3 pounds new potatoes, washed and halved
12 slices bacon, chopped
2 tablespoons white wine
Salt and pepper
1 rosemary sprig

Directions:
1. Put the wine, potatoes, and rosemary in your slow cooker.
2. Add salt and pepper and top with chopped bacon.
3. Cook for 3 hours on high.
4. Serve the potatoes warm.

Bean Queso

Time: 6 hrs 15 mins　　　**Servings: 10**

Ingredients:
1 can black beans, drained
1 cup chopped green chiles
1/2 cup red salsa
1 teaspoon dried oregano
1/2 teaspoon cumin powder
1 cup light beer
1 1/2 cups grated Cheddar
Salt and pepper to taste

Directions:
1. Put the oregano, cumin, salsa, beer, beans, chiles, and cheese in your slow cooker.
2. Add salt and pepper and cook on low for 6 hours.
3. Serve the bean queso warm.

Pizza Dip

Time: 6 hrs 15 mins　　**Servings: 20**

Ingredients:
1 onion, chopped
1/2 pound salami, diced
2 garlic cloves, minced
2 cups tomato sauce
1/2 cup grated Parmesan
1 cup shredded mozzarella
1/2 teaspoon dried basil
1/2 teaspoon dried oregano
1 pound spicy sausages, sliced
1 red bell pepper, cored and diced
1 yellow bell pepper, cored and sliced

Directions:
1. Place all the ingredients in your slow cooker.
2. Cook for 6 hours on low, stirring once during cooking to make sure that the ingredients are properly mixed.
3. Serve the pizza dip warm.

Green Vegetable Dip

Time: 2 hrs 15 mins　　　**Servings: 12**

Ingredients
10 oz. frozen spinach, thawed and drained
1 jar artichoke hearts, drained
1 cup chopped parsley
1 cup cream cheese
1 cup sour cream
1/2 cup grated Parmesan cheese
1/2 cup feta cheese, crumbled
1/2 teaspoon onion powder
1/4 teaspoon garlic powder

Directions:
1. Put all the ingredients in your slow cooker and mix gently.
2. Cover and cook for 2 hours on high.
3. Serve the dip hot or cold with crackers, crusty bread, other salty snacks, or vegetable sticks.

Spicy Enchilada Dip

Time: 6 hrs 15 mins   **Servings: 8**

Ingredients:
1 pound ground chicken
1/2 teaspoon chili powder
1 shallot, chopped
2 garlic cloves, chopped
1 red bell pepper, cored and diced
2 tomatoes, diced
1 cup tomato sauce
Salt and pepper
1 1/2 cups grated cheddar cheese

Directions:
1. Put the ground chicken with shallot, chili powder, and garlic in your slow cooker.
2. Add the remaining ingredients and cook for 6 hours on low.
3. Serve the dip warm with tortilla chips.

Mixed Olive Dip

Time: 1 hr 45 mins   **Servings: 10**

Ingredients:
1 pound ground chicken
2 tablespoons olive oil
1 green bell pepper, cored and diced
1/2 cup Kalamata olives, pitted and chopped
1/2 cup green olives, chopped
1/2 cup black olives, pitted and chopped
1 cup green salsa
1/2 cup chicken stock
1 cup grated cheddar cheese
1/2 cup shredded mozzarella cheese

Directions:
1. Put all the ingredients in your slow cooker.
2. Cover and cook for 1 hour 30 mins on high.
3. Serve the dip warm.

Spicy Asian Style Mushrooms

Time: 2 hrs 15 mins   **Servings: 8**

Ingredients:
1/4 cup hoisin sauce
1/4 cup soy sauce
2 garlic cloves, minced
1/2 teaspoon red pepper flakes
2 pounds fresh mushrooms, cleaned

Directions:
1. Combine the soy sauce, garlic, hoisin sauce, and red pepper flakes in a bowl.
2. Put the mushrooms in the slow cooker and drizzle them with the sauce.
3. Cook for 2 hours on high.
4. Let the mushroom cool in the pot before serving.

Three-Cheese Artichoke Sauce

Time: 4 hrs 15 mins   **Servings: 16**

Ingredients:
1 jar artichoke hearts, drained and chopped
1 shallot, chopped
2 cups shredded mozzarella cheese
1 cup grated Parmesan cheese
1 cup grated Swiss cheese
1/2 teaspoon dried thyme
1/4 teaspoon chili powder

Directions:
1. Put all the ingredients in your slow cooker.
2. Cover the pot and cook for 4 hours on low setting.
3. Serve the sauce warm with vegetable sticks, crackers, or small pretzels.

Mexican Chili Dip

Time: 2 hrs 15 mins   **Servings: 20**

Ingredients:
1 can black beans, drained
1/2 cup beef stock
Salt and pepper
1 can diced tomatoes
1/2 teaspoon cumin powder
1 can red beans, drained
1/2 teaspoon chili powder
1 1/2 cups grated cheddar cheese

Directions
1. Put tomatoes, cumin powder, beans, chili, and stock in your slow cooker.
2. Add salt and pepper and top with grated cheese.
3. Cook for 2 hours on high.
4. Serve the dip warm.

Spicy Glazed Pecans

Time: 3 hrs 15 mins   **Servings: 10**

Ingredients:
1 teaspoon dried thyme
2 pounds pecans
1/2 teaspoon garlic powder
2 tablespoons honey
1 teaspoon smoked paprika
1 teaspoon dried basil
1/2 cup butter, melted
1 teaspoon chili powder
1/4 teaspoon cayenne pepper

Directions:
1. Put all the ingredients in your slow cooker.
2. Mix well until they are well combined and the pecans are evenly glazed.
3. Cook for 3 hours on high.
4. Allow to cool before serving.

Boiled Peanuts with Skin On

Time: 7 hrs 15 mins   **Servings: 8**

Ingredients:
4 cups water
1/2 cup salt
2 pounds uncooked, whole peanuts

Directions:
1. Put all the ingredients in your slow cooker.
2. Cover and cook for 7 hours on low.
3. Drain and allow to cool down before serving.

Cheesy Mushroom Dip

Time: 4 hrs 15 mins   **Servings: 16**

Ingredients:
1/2 teaspoon chili powder
1 pound mushrooms, chopped
1 teaspoon Worcestershire sauce
1 cup grated Swiss cheese
1/4 cup evaporated milk
1 can condensed cream of mushroom soup
1 cup grated cheddar cheese

Directions:
1. Mix the cream of mushroom soup, evaporated milk, mushrooms, Worcestershire sauce, and chili powder in your slow cooker.
2. Top with grated cheese and cook for 4 hours on low.
3. Serve the dip warm or reheated.

Taco Dip

Time: 6 hrs 30 mins   **Servings: 20**

Ingredients:
2 pounds ground beef
2 tablespoons canola oil
1 can black beans, drained
1/2 cup beef stock
1 cup tomato sauce
1 tablespoon taco seasoning
2 cups Velveeta cheese, shredded

Directions:
1. Place a pan over medium heat and add the beef. Cook for 10 minutes, stirring often.
2. Put the beef in your slow cooker.
3. Add the remaining ingredients and cook for 6 hours on low.
4. Serve the dip warm.

Swiss Cheese Fondue

Time: 4 hrs 15 mins   **Servings: 10**

Ingredients:
1 garlic cloves
2 cups dry white wine
2 cups grated Swiss cheese
1 cup grated cheddar cheese
2 tablespoons cornstarch
1 pinch nutmeg

Directions:
1. Rub the interior part of your slow cooker with a garlic clove. Dispose of the clove once done.
2. Add all the ingredients and cook for 4 hours on low heat.
3. Serve the fondue warm with croutons, vegetable sticks, or pretzels.

Quick Layered Appetizer

Time: 7 hrs 30 mins   **Servings: 10**

Ingredients:
4 chicken breasts, cooked and diced
1 teaspoon dried basil
1 teaspoon dried oregano
1 cup cream cheese
1/4 teaspoon chili powder
Salt and pepper
4 tomatoes, sliced
4 large tortillas
2 cups shredded mozzarella

Directions:
1. Mix the chili powder, salt, oregano, cream cheese, chicken, basil, and pepper in a bowl.
2. Begin layering the chicken mixture, tomatoes, tortillas and mozzarella in your slow cooker.
3. Cover and cook for 7 hours on low.
4. Let it cool, then slice and serve.

Oriental Chicken Bites

Time: 7 hrs 15 mins   **Servings: 10**

Ingredients:
1 teaspoon smoked paprika
2 tablespoons olive oil
Salt and pepper to taste
1 teaspoon grated ginger
4 garlic cloves, minced
2 sweet onions, sliced
1/2 lemon, juiced
1 teaspoon cumin powder
1 cup chicken stock
4 chicken breasts, cubed
1/2 teaspoon cinnamon powder

Directions:
1. Put all the ingredients in your slow cooker.
2. Add salt and pepper and mix well until the ingredients are completely distributed.
3. Cover and cook for 7 hours on low.
4. Serve the chicken bites hot or cold.

Sweet Corn Jalapeno Dip

Time: 2 hrs 15 mins   **Servings: 10**

Ingredients:
1 pinch nutmeg
2 tablespoons chopped cilantro
4 bacon slices, chopped
1 cup sour cream
1 cup grated cheddar cheese
1/2 cup cream cheese
3 cans sweet corn, drained
4 jalapenos, seeded and chopped

Directions:
1. Put the corn, jalapenos, sour cream, cheddar cheese, cream cheese and nutmeg in a slow cooker.
2. Cook on high for 2 hours.
3. When done, stir in the cilantro and serve the dip warm.

Pretzel Party Mix

Time: 2 hrs 15 mins   **Servings: 10**

Ingredients:
1 teaspoon salt
1 teaspoon garlic powder
1 teaspoon Worcestershire sauce
4 cups pretzels
1 cup crispy rice cereals
1/4 cup butter, melted
1 cup peanuts
1 cup pecans

Directions:
1. Put the pretzels, peanuts, pecans and rice cereals in your slow cooker.
2. Add melted butter and Worcestershire sauce and mix well, then add salt and garlic powder.
3. Cover and cook the mixture for 2 hours on high. Stir once during cooking.
4. Let it cool before serving.

Maple Syrup Glazed Carrots

Time: 6 hrs 15 mins   **Servings: 8**

Ingredients:
1 teaspoon salt
4 tablespoons butter, melted
3 tablespoons maple syrup
3 pounds baby carrots
1/8 teaspoon pumpkin pie spice

Directions:
1. Place the baby carrots in your slow cooker and add the remaining ingredients.
2. Stir until the carrots are completely coated.
3. Cover and cook for 6 hours on low.
4. Serve the carrots hot or cold.

Balsamic Pulled Pork

Time: 8 hrs 15 mins   **Servings: 6**

Ingredients:
1/4 cup balsamic vinegar
2 tablespoons soy sauce
1/4 cup hoisin sauce
2 garlic cloves, minced
2 shallots, sliced
1 tablespoon Dijon mustard
2 pounds boneless pork shoulder
2 tablespoons honey
1/4 cup chicken stock

Directions

Put the stock, garlic, shallots, honey, hoisin sauce, vinegar, mustard, and soy sauce in your slow cooker.
2. Add the pork shoulder and stir in the mixture until completely coated.
3. Cover and cook for 8 hours on low.
4. Cut the meat into fine pieces and serve hot or cold.

Cheesy Beef Dip

Time: 3 hrs 15 mins   **Servings: 8**

Ingredients:
2 pounds ground beef
1 pound grated cheddar cheese
1/2 cup cream cheese
1/2 cup white wine
1 poblano pepper, chopped

Directions:
1. Put all the ingredients in a crock pot.
2. Cook for 3 hours on high.
3. Serve the dip warm.

Bacon Black Bean Dip

Time: 6 hrs 15 mins   **Servings: 6**

Ingredients:
2 shallots, sliced
1 garlic cloves, chopped
2 cans black beans, drained
1/2 cup beef stock
1 tablespoon brown sugar
2 tablespoons Bourbon
Salt and pepper
1 tablespoon molasses
1/2 teaspoon chili powder
1 cup red salsa
6 bacon slices
1 tablespoon apple cider vinegar

Directions:
1. Place a saucepan over medium heat and add the bacon. Cook until crisp, then place the bacon and its fat in your crockpot.
2. Add all other ingredients
3. Cook for 6 hours on low.
4. When done, partially mash the beans and serve immediately.

Spicy Monterey Jack Fondue

Time: 4 hrs 15 mins   **Servings: 6**

Ingredients:
1 pinch salt
1 pinch ground black pepper
2 cups grated Monterey Jack cheese
1 garlic clove
1 cup white wine
1 red chili, seeded and chopped
1 tablespoon cornstarch
1/2 cup grated Parmesan cheese
1/2 cup milk
1 pinch nutmeg

Directions:
1. Rub the interior part of your slow cooker's pot with a garlic clove just to infuse it with aroma.
2. Put the white wine in the pot then add the cornstarch, red chili, cheeses, and milk.
3. Add salt, nutmeg, and black pepper and cook for 4 hours on low heat.
4. Serve the fondue warm with bread cubes or vegetables.

Tahini Cheese Dip

Time: 2 hrs 15 mins   **Servings: 8**

Ingredients:
1 pinch nutmeg
1/4 cup grated Emmentaler cheese
Salt and pepper
1/2 cup tahini paste
1/2 teaspoon cumin powder
1/4 pound grated Gruyère cheese
1 cup whole milk
1/8 teaspoon garlic powder

Directions:
1. Put all the ingredients in your crockpot.
2. Add salt and pepper to taste and cover the pot.
3. Cook for 2 hours on high.
4. Serve the dip warm.

Tahini Chickpea Dip

Time: 6 hrs 15 mins   **Servings: 6**

Ingredients:
2 cups dried chickpeas, rinsed
5 cups water
1 bay leaf
Salt and pepper
1 lemon, juiced
1/4 cup tahini paste
2 tablespoons olive oil
1 pinch red pepper flakes

Directions:
1. Put the water, salt, bay leaf, chickpeas, and pepper in a slow cooker.
2. Cook for 6 hours on low then drain and transfer in the blender.
3. Add the remaining ingredients and blend until smooth.
4. Serve the dip fresh or store in an airtight container in the fridge.

Roasted Bell Peppers Dip

Time: 2 hrs 15 mins   **Servings: 8**

Ingredients:
4 roasted red bell peppers, drained
2 cans chickpeas, drained
1/2 cup water
1 shallot, chopped
4 garlic cloves, minced
Salt and pepper
2 tablespoons lemon juice
2 tablespoons olive oil

Directions:
1. Put the chickpeas, shallot, water, bell peppers, and garlic in a slow cooker.
2. Add salt and pepper as required and cook for 2 hours on high.
3. When done, purèe the dip in a food processor. Add the lemon juice and olive oil.
4. Serve, or store in fridge in an airtight container for up to 2 days.

French Onion Dip

Time: 4 hrs 15 mins   **Servings: 10**

Ingredients:
4 large onions, chopped
2 tablespoons olive oil
1 tablespoon butter
1 1/2 cups sour cream
1 pinch nutmeg
Salt and pepper

Directions:
1. Put the pepper, salt, olive oil, butter, onions, and nutmeg in a slow cooker.
2. Cover and cook on high for 4 hours.
3. When done, let cool, then add the sour cream, salt, and pepper.
4. Serve the dip immediately.

Pimiento Cheese Dip

Tim: 2 hrs 15 mins   **Servings: 6**

Ingredients:
1/2 pound grated cheddar
1/4 pound grated pepper Jack cheese
1/2 cup sour cream
1/2 cup green olives, sliced
2 tablespoons diced pimientos
1 teaspoon hot sauce
1/4 teaspoon garlic powder
1/4 teaspoon onion powder

Directions:
1. Put all the ingredients in a slow cooker.
2. Cover the pot and cook for 2 hours on high.
3. Serve the dip warm with vegetable sticks or breadsticks.

Eggplant Caviar

Time: 3 hrs 15 mins   **Servings: 6**

Ingredients:
2 garlic cloves, minced
Salt and pepper
1 teaspoon dried oregano
1 lemon, juiced
2 large eggplants, peeled and cubed
4 tablespoons olive oil
1 teaspoon dried basil

Directions:
1. Put the olive oil, basil, eggplant cubes, and oregano in a slow cooker.
2. Add salt and pepper and cook for 3 hours on high.
3. When done, add the garlic, lemon juice, salt and pepper. Mash and mix well with a potato masher.
4. Serve the dip cool.

Bacon Baked Potatoes

Time: 3 hrs 15 mins   **Servings: 8**

Ingredients:
1 teaspoon dried rosemary
Salt and pepper
1/4 cup chicken stock
3 pounds new potatoes, halved
8 slices bacon, chopped

Directions:
1. Place a pan over medium heat and add the bacon. Cook until crisp; do not drain.
2. Put the potatoes in a slow cooker. Add the bacon bits and fat, and also rosemary, salt and pepper and stir until completely mixed
3. Add the stock and cook for 3 hours on high heat.
4. Serve the potatoes warm.

Sausage and Pepper Appetizer

Time: 6 hrs 15 mins   **Servings: 8**

Ingredients:
Salt and pepper
4 roasted bell peppers, chopped
1 poblano pepper, chopped
6 fresh pork sausages, skins removed
1 can fire roasted tomatoes
1 cup grated Provolone cheese
2 tablespoons olive oil
1 shallot, chopped

Directions:
1. Add the oil to a frying pan. Add the sausage meat and cook for 5 minutes, stirring often.
2. Transfer the meat to your slow cooker and add the remaining ingredients.
3. Season with salt and pepper and cook on low for 6 hours.
4. Serve the dish hot or cold.

Teriyaki Chicken Wings

Time: 6 hrs 15 mins   **Servings: 6**

Ingredients:
1/2 cup pineapple juice
1/4 cup water
2 tablespoons canola oil
1/2 teaspoon garlic powder
1/2 teaspoon ground ginger
2 tablespoons brown sugar
1 tablespoon molasses
1/2 cup soy sauce
3 pounds chicken wings

Directions:
1. Put all the ingredients in a slow cooker and mix until chicken is completely coated.
2. Cover the pot and cook for 6 hours on low.
3. Serve the chicken wings hot or cold.

Goat Cheese Stuffed Mushrooms

Time: 4 hrs 15 mins   **Servings: 6**

Ingredients:
1 egg
1 teaspoon dried oregano
1/2 cup breadcrumbs
12 medium size mushrooms
6 oz. goat cheese
1 poblano pepper, chopped

Directions:
1. Combine the egg, breadcrumbs, goat cheese, pepper and oregano in a bowl.
2. Coat each mushroom with the goat cheese mixture and put them in a slow cooker.
3. Cover and cook the mixture for 4 hours on low.
4. Serve the mushrooms hot or cold.

Pepperoni Pizza Dip

Time: 3 hrs 15 mins   **Servings: 10**

Ingredients:
1 cup cream cheese
2 red bell peppers, diced
1 cup shredded mozzarella
2 shallots, chopped
1/2 teaspoon dried basil
1/2 cup black olives
1 1/2 cups pizza sauce
4 peperoni, sliced

Directions:
1. Mix the pizza sauce and the remaining ingredients in your slow cooker.
2. Cover the pot and cook for 3 hours on low.
3. Serve the dip warm with breadsticks or tortilla chips.

Creamy Potatoes

Time: 6 hrs 15 mins   **Servings: 6**

Ingredients:
2 green onions, chopped   1 shallot, chopped
4 bacon slices, chopped   2 garlic cloves, chopped
Salt and pepper   2 tablespoons olive oil
1 cup sour cream
1 teaspoon dried oregano
3 pounds small new potatoes, washed
2 tablespoons chopped parsley
Directions:

1. Put the bacon, oregano, potatoes, shallot, olive oil and garlic in a slow cooker.
2. Add salt and pepper and stir until the ingredients are evenly distributed.
3. Cover the pot and cook for 6 hours on low.
4. When done, mix the potatoes with sour cream, onions, and parsley and serve immediately.

Beer Cheese Fondue

Time: 2 hrs 15 mins   **Servings: 8**

Ingredients:
1 shallot, chopped   1 garlic clove, minced
1 cup grated Gruyère cheese 2 cups grated cheddar
1 tablespoon cornstarch   1 cup beer
1 teaspoon Dijon mustard   Salt and pepper
1/2 teaspoon cumin seeds

Directions:
1. Put the cumin seeds, cheeses, cornstarch, shallot, garlic, mustard, and beer in your slow cooker.
2. Add salt and pepper and mix well.
3. Cover the pot and cook for 2 hours on high.
4. Serve the fondue warm.

CHAPTER 2

CHICKEN RECIPES

Orange Glazed Chicken

Time: 6 hrs. 15 mins.   **Servings: 6**

Ingredients:

1 cup vegetable stock
1 orange, zested and juiced
1/4 tsp. cumin powder
1 tbsp. balsamic vinegar
1 tbsp. cornstarch
2 sweet onions, sliced
1/2 tsp. Worcestershire sauce

Salt and pepper
6 chicken thighs
2 tbsp. olive oil

Directions:

1. Put the chicken, orange zest, orange juice, olive oil, onions, stock, cornstarch, balsamic vinegar, Worcestershire sauce and cumin powder in your crock pot.
2. Add salt and pepper and cook the chicken for 6 hours on low.
3. Serve warm.

Chicken Barley Squash Salad

Time: 6 hrs. 15 mins.   **Servings: 8**

Ingredients:

1-lb. ground chicken
1 cup pearl barley
2 cups vegetable stock
2 tbsp. chopped parsley
Salt and pepper to taste.
2 cups butternut squash cubes

2 garlic cloves, chopped.
1 cup green peas
1 sweet onion, chopped.
2 tbsp. olive oil
Lemon juice for serving

Directions:

1. Place a saucepan over medium heat and add the bacon and chicken. Cook for a few minutes then place in your crock pot.
2. Add the remaining ingredients, and salt and pepper.
3. Cook for 6 hours on low.
4. Serve the salad warm and fresh, drizzled with lemon juice.

BBQ Chicken

Time: 8 hrs. 15 mins.   **Servings: 8**

Ingredients:

1/2 tsp. chili powder
2 tbsp. lemon juice
1 cup BBQ sauce
1 tsp. mustard seeds
Salt and pepper
4 chicken breasts, boneless and skinless, halved

1 tsp. Worcestershire sauce
2 tbsp. maple syrup
1/2 cup vegetable stock
1/2 tsp. garlic powder

Directions:

1. Put all the ingredients in your crock pot.
2. Add salt and pepper to taste and cook for 8 hours on low.
3. Serve the chicken warm with your favorite side dish.

Multigrain Chicken Pilaf

Time: 6 hrs. 30 mins.   Servings: 8

Ingredients:

2 cups vegetable stock
1 cup green peas
1/2 cup pearl barley
2 garlic cloves, chopped
1/2 tsp. dried sage
2 chicken breasts, cubed
1 sweet potato, peeled and cubed
1 tbsp. chopped parsley for serving

1 cup frozen edamame
1/2 cup wild rice
1 leek, sliced
Salt and pepper
1/2 tsp. dried oregano

Directions:

1. Put the stock, sage, chicken, leek, garlic, edamame, green peas, sweet potatoes, wild rice, pearl barley, and oregano in your crock pot.
2. Add salt and pepper to taste and cook for 6 hours on low.
3. When done, add the parsley and serve warm.

Cream Cheese Chicken

Time: 4 hrs. 15 mins.   Servings: 4
Ingredients:
1/2 cup chicken stock
1 sweet onion, chopped
4 chicken breasts
1-can cream of chicken soup
1 tsp. dried Italian herbs
1 cup cream cheese
4 garlic cloves, minced
2 tbsp. butter
Salt and pepper

Directions:
1. Add salt, pepper, and Italian herbs to the Chicken. Dissolve the butter in a saucepan and add the chicken. Cook and then place the chicken in your crock pot.
2. Add the remaining ingredients and adjust the taste with salt and pepper.
3. Cook on low for 4 hours. Serve warm.

Chicken Sweet Potato Stew

Time: 3 hrs. 15 mins.   Servings: 6
Ingredients:
2 tbsp. butter
2 shallots, chopped
1 pinch cinnamon powder
1½ cups vegetable stock
1/2 tsp. cumin powder
2 chicken breasts, cubed
2-lbs. sweet potatoes, peeled and cubed
1/2 tsp. garlic powder
Salt and pepper to taste

Directions:
1. Put the butter, chicken, and shallots in your crock pot. Cook for 5 minutes then place in your crock pot.
2. Add the sweet potatoes, cumin powder, garlic and cinnamon, as well as stock, salt and pepper.
3. Cook for 3 hours on high. Serve the stew hot or cold.

Adobo Chicken with Bok Choy

Time: 6 hrs. 30 mins.   Servings: 4
Ingredients:
4 chicken breasts
1 cup chicken stock
4 garlic cloves, minced
1 sweet onion, chopped
1 head bok choy, shredded
2 tbsp. soy sauce
1 tbsp. brown sugar
1 tsp. paprika

Directions:
1. Put the paprika, onion, soy sauce, chicken, garlic, brown sugar, and stock in your crock pot.
2. Cook for 4 hours on low, then add the bok choy. Continue cooking for another 2 hours.
3. Serve warm.

Chicken Taco Filling

Time: 6 hrs. 15 mins.   Servings: 8
Ingredients:
1/2 tsp. celery seeds
1/2 tsp. cumin powder
1 tbsp. taco seasoning
1/4 tsp. chili powder
4 chicken breasts, halved
1 cup chicken stock

Directions:
1. Put all the ingredients in your crock pot. Add salt and pepper to taste.
2. Cook for 6 hours on low.
3. When done, shred the meat into fine threads and serve it in taco shells.

Paprika Chicken Wings

Time: 3 hrs. 15 mins.   Servings: 4
Ingredients:
Salt and pepper
2-lbs. chicken wings
1½ tsp. smoked paprika
1 tbsp. honey
1/2 tsp. sweet paprika
1/2 cup chicken stock.

Directions:
1. Put the honey, salt, chicken wings, paprika, and pepper in your crock pot.
2. Add the stock then cover and cook for 3 hours on high.
3. Serve the chicken warm and fresh with your favorite side dish.

Red Wine Chicken and Mushroom Stew

Time: 6 hrs. 30 mins.   Servings: 6
Ingredients:
1 large onion, chopped
4 garlic cloves, minced
1 bay leaf
1 thyme sprig
Salt and pepper
6 chicken thighs
4 cups sliced mushrooms
1/2 cup red wine
1 cup chicken stock

Directions:
1. Put the stock, bay leaf, onion, garlic, mushrooms, chicken, red wine, and thyme in your crock pot.
2. Add salt and pepper to taste and cook for 6 hours on low.
3. Serve the stew warm and fresh.

Curry Braised Chicken

Time: 8 hrs. 15 mins.   Servings: 6
Ingredients:
1/2 tsp. cumin powder
1 tsp. curry powder
Salt and pepper
1 cup chicken stock
6 chicken thighs
1/4 tsp. chili powder
1/2 tsp. onion powder
1 tsp. garlic powder
1 tbsp. grated ginger
1/2 cup plain yogurt
Cooked white rice for serving

Directions:
1. Combine the chicken with onion, curry powder, garlic powder, cumin, ginger, and chili powder.
2. Transfer the chicken to the crock pot then add the yogurt and stock.
3. Add salt and pepper and cook for 8 hours on low.
4. Serve the chicken warm with cooked white rice.

Chicken Layered Potato Casserole

Time: 6 hrs. 30 mins.   Servings: 8
Ingredients:
2-lbs. potatoes, peeled and sliced
1 cup heavy cream
1½ cups whole milk
2 chicken breasts, cut into thin strips
1/4 tsp. chili powder
1/4 tsp. onion powder
1/4 tsp. cumin powder
1/2 tsp. garlic powder
Salt and pepper to taste

Directions:
1. Put the cumin powder, garlic powder, cream, milk, chili powder, and onion powder.
2. Place the potatoes and chicken in your slow cooker.
3. Pour the milk mixture over the potatoes and chicken then add salt and pepper.
4. Cook for 6 hours on low. Serve the casserole hot or cold.

Greek Orzo Chicken

Time: 6 hrs. 30 mins.   Servings: 6
Ingredients:
Salt and pepper
2 chicken breasts, cubed
1 celery stalk, diced
1/2 tsp. dried basil
1 tsp. dried oregano
2 ripe tomatoes, peeled and diced
1/4 cup pitted Kalamata olives
2 cups chicken stock
1/2 tsp. dried parsley
1 cup orzo, rinsed
Feta cheese for serving

Directions:
1. Place the orzo and the remaining ingredients in the crock pot.
2. Add salt and pepper to taste and cook for 6 hours on low.
3. Serve the chicken warm and top with feta cheese.

Spiced Butter Chicken

Time: 6 hrs. 45 mins.   Servings: 6
Ingredients:

6 chicken thighs	1 large onion, chopped.
4 garlic cloves, chopped	1½ cups coconut milk
2 tbsp. butter	1 tsp. curry powder
1 tsp. garam masala	1/2 tsp. cumin powder
1/4 tsp. chili powder	Salt and pepper
1/2 cup plain yogurt for serving	

Directions:
1. Heat the butter in the slow cooker. Add the chicken and cook until it turns golden brown.
2. Place the chicken in your slow cooker and add the remaining ingredients.
3. Cook for 6 hours on low.
4. Serve the chicken warm.

Garden Chicken Stew

Time: 8 hrs. 30 mins.   Servings: 8
Ingredients:
1 onion, chopped
1 tsp. dried oregano
1 cup tomato sauce
2 cups chicken stock
4 large potatoes, peeled and cubed
2 carrots, sliced
1/2 tsp. dried basil
3 chicken breasts, cubed
1-can (15 oz. white beans, drained
2 tbsp. canola oil
2 celery stalks, sliced
2 ripe tomatoes, peeled and diced
Salt and pepper to taste

Directions:
1. Put all the ingredients in your crock pot.
2. Add salt and pepper and cook the stew for 8 hours on low until the chicken and veggies are tender.
3. Serve the stew warm.

Spiced Chicken over Wild Rice

Time: 7 hrs. 15 mins.   Servings: 6
Ingredients:
2 cups sliced mushrooms
2 celery stalk, diced
6 chicken thighs
1 carrot, diced
1/2 tsp. chili powder
Salt and pepper to taste
2 cups vegetable stock
1 cup wild rice
1 tsp. cumin powder

Directions:
1. Sprinkle the chicken with salt, cumin powder, chili, and pepper.
2. Put the carrot, mushrooms, stock, rice, celery, salt, and pepper in your crock pot.
3. Place the chicken on top and cook for 7 hours on low.
4. Serve the chicken and rice warm or chilled.

Turmeric Chicken Stew

Time: 6 hrs. 30 mins.   Servings: 6
Ingredients:

1 cup tomato sauce	1 cup coconut milk
1 cup chicken stock	Salt and pepper
2 tbsp. canola oil	1 tsp. turmeric powder

2 chicken breasts, cubed
15 oz. chickpeas, drained.
2 red bell peppers, cored and diced
2 cups fresh spinach, shredded
1/2 head cauliflower, cut into florets

Directions:
1. Season the chicken with salt, pepper, and turmeric powder.
2. Heat the canola oil in a pan and add the chicken; cook for a few minutes until golden.
3. Place the chicken in your slow cooker then add the remaining ingredients.
4. Sprinkle with salt and pepper and cook for 6 hours on low. Serve warm.

Honey Garlic Chicken Thighs with Snap Peas

Time: 6 hrs. 15 mins.   Servings: 6
Ingredients:

6 chicken thighs	1 lb. snap peas
1/4 cup vegetable	2 tbsp. soy sauce
stock 3 tbsp. honey	1/2 tsp. cumin powder
1/2 tsp. smoked paprika	1/2 tsp. fennel seeds

Directions:
1. Put the cumin powder, paprika, chicken, honey, fennel seeds, and soy sauce in a bowl and mix well.
2. Combine the snap peas and stock in your crock pot.
3. Place the chicken over the snap peas and cover.
4. Cook for 6 hours on low.
5. Serve the chicken and snap peas warm.

Vegetable Braised Chicken

Time: 7 hrs. 30 mins.   Servings: 8
Ingredients:
1 rosemary sprig
2 cups vegetable stock
Salt and pepper
2 carrots, sliced
2 celery stalks, sliced
1 parsnip, sliced
4 chicken breasts, cut into smaller pieces
1 thyme sprig
2 large potatoes, peeled and cubed

Directions:
1. Put all the ingredients in your slow cooker. Add salt and pepper; cover.
2. Cook for 7 hours on low.
3. Serve the chicken warm.

Parmesan Chicken

Time: 6 hrs. 15 mins.   Servings: 4
Ingredients:
1½ cups grated Parmesan
1/2 tsp. cumin powder
4 chicken breasts
1/2 cup chicken stock
1/4 tsp. chili powder
1 tsp. dried thyme
Salt and pepper

Directions:
1. Put the chicken with salt, cumin powder, chili powder, pepper, and thyme in the crock pot.
2. Add the stock to the pot and top the chicken with grated cheese.
3. Cook for 6 hours on low.
4. Serve the chicken warm.

Cider Braised Chicken

Time: 8 hrs. 15 mins.   Servings: 8
Ingredients:
1 tsp. cumin powder
Salt and pepper
1½ cups apple cider
1 tsp. dried thyme
1 whole chicken, cut into smaller pieces
1 tsp. dried oregano

Directions:
1. Sprinkle the chicken with oregano, salt, thyme, and cumin powder and put it in your crock pot.
2. Add the apple cider and cook for 8 hours on low.
3. Serve the chicken warm with your favorite dish.

Soy Braised Chicken

Time: 3 hrs. 15 mins.   Servings: 6
Ingredients:
1/4 cup apple cider
2 shallots, sliced.
1 bay leaf
1/2 tsp. cayenne pepper
Salt and pepper to taste
1/4 cup soy sauce
6 chicken thighs
2 garlic cloves, chopped
1 tbsp. brown sugar
Cooked white rice for serving

Directions:
1. Put the chicken, apple cider, soy sauce, shallots, garlic cloves, leaf, brown sugar, and cayenne pepper in the crock pot.
2. Add salt and pepper to taste and cook for 3 hours on high.
3. Serve the chicken warm.

Chicken Black Olive Stew

Time: 6 hrs. 15 mins.   Servings: 6
Ingredients:
1/4 tsp. chili powder
6 chicken thighs
1/2 cup tomato sauce
1/4 cup dry white wine
2 tbsp. tomato paste
1/2 cup pitted black olives
1/2 cup pitted Kalamata olives
1 shallot, chopped.
1-can (28 oz.) diced tomatoes
2 tbsp. olive oil
4 garlic cloves, minced
Salt and pepper

Directions:
1. Put all the ingredients in your crock pot, adding salt and pepper to taste.
2. Cook for 6 hours on low.
3. Serve the stew warm.

Fennel Braised Chicken

Time: 6 hrs. 15 mins.   Servings: 4
Ingredients:
2 oranges, juiced
1 bay leaf
4 chicken breasts
2 carrots, sliced
1 sweet onion, sliced
Salt and pepper to taste
1½ cups chicken stock
1 fennel bulb, sliced

Directions:
1. Put all the ingredients in your crock pot.
2. Add salt and pepper and cook for 6 hours on low.
3. Serve the chicken warm.

Korean BBQ Chicken

Time: 3 hrs. 15 mins.   Servings: 4
Ingredients:
1/2 cup chicken stock
1 green onion, chopped
1 tsp. chili paste
4 boneless and skinless chicken breasts
2 tbsp. brown sugar
1 tbsp. rice vinegar
6 garlic cloves, minced
1/4 cup soy sauce
1 tsp. grated ginger

Directions:
1. Combine the chicken and the remaining ingredients in the crock pot.
2. Cover and cook for 3 hours on high.
3. Serve the chicken warm.

White Chicken Cassoulet

Time: 6 hrs. 15 mins.   Servings: 8
Ingredients:
2 carrots, sliced
1 cup chicken stock
1 large onion, chopped
2 garlic cloves, chopped
1/4 cup dry white wine
2 celery stalks, sliced
2 tbsp. canola oil
Salt and pepper
4 chicken breasts, cubed
2 cans (15 oz. each) white beans

Directions:
1. Heat the oil in a pan and add the chicken.
2. Fry for a few minutes until golden then place the chicken in the slow cooker.
3. Add the remaining ingredients to your crock pot and add salt and pepper.
4. Cook for 6 hours on low.
5. Serve the cassoulet warm.

Medley Vegetable Chicken Stew

Time: 8 hrs. 15 mins.   Servings: 8
Ingredients:
2 sweet potatoes, peeled and cubed
1-can (15 oz.) chickpeas, drained
1 cup vegetable stock
1/2 tsp. chili powder
1/2 tsp. dried oregano
Salt and pepper to taste
2 carrots, sliced
1-can fire roasted tomatoes
8 chicken drumsticks
1 onion, chopped.
4 garlic cloves, chopped
1 celery stalk, sliced
1/2 tsp. cumin powder

Directions:
1. Put the chicken, vegetables, spices, and stock in the crock pot.
2. Sprinkle with salt and pepper and cook for 8 hours on low.
3. Serve the stew warm and fresh.

Chicken Cauliflower Gratin

Time: 6 hrs. 15 mins.   Servings: 6
Ingredients:
1½ cups grated cheddar
2 chicken breasts, cubed
1 pinch cayenne pepper
Salt and pepper
1/2 tsp. garlic powder
1 head cauliflower, cut into florets
1 can condensed cream of chicken soup

Directions:
1. Put the chicken soup, salt, garlic powder, cayenne pepper, cauliflower, chicken, and pepper in your crock pot.
2. Top with grated cheese and cook for 6 hours on low.
3. Serve the dish warm.

Chicken Tikka Masala

Time: 2 hrs. 30 mins.   Servings: 4
Ingredients:
4 chicken thighs
1 cup coconut milk
1 cup diced tomatoes
1 lime, juiced
2 tbsp. tomato paste
Chopped cilantro for serving
1/2 cup chicken stock
2 shallots, chopped
4 garlic cloves, minced
Cooked rice for serving
1 tbsp. garam masala
2 tbsp. canola oil
Salt and pepper
Directions:
1. Heat the oil in a pan and add the chicken. Cook until golden, then place the chicken in your slow cooker.
2. Add the remaining ingredients and sprinkle with salt and pepper.
3. Cook for 2 hours on high.
4. Serve the dish warm, topped with chopped cilantro, over cooked rice.

Sesame Glazed Chicken

Time: 3 hrs. 15 mins.   Servings: 6
Ingredients:
2 tbsp. fresh orange juice
2 tbsp. hoisin sauce
1 tsp. grated ginger
2 tbsp. water
1 tbsp. sesame seeds
6 chicken thighs
1 tbsp. cornstarch
1 tbsp. sesame oil
2 tbsp. soy sauce
1 tbsp. brown sugar

Directions:
1. Put all the ingredients in your crock pot.
2. Cook for 3 hours on high.
3. Serve warm with your favorite side dish.

Cheesy Chicken

Time: 2 hrs. 15 mins.   Servings: 2
Ingredients:
1 cup cream of chicken soup
1/4 tsp. garlic powder
2 chicken breasts
1 cup grated cheddar
Salt and pepper

Directions:
1. Put all the remaining ingredients in the crock pot.
2. Add salt and pepper to taste; cover.
3. Cook for 2 hours on high.
4. Serve the chicken warm, topped with plenty of cheesy sauce.

Tomato Soy Glazed Chicken

Time: 8 hrs. 15 mins.   Servings: 8
Ingredients:
1/2 cup tomato sauce
2 tbsp. brown sugar
8 chicken thighs
1/2 cup soy sauce
1 tsp. chili powder

Directions:
1. Put all the ingredients in your crock pot.
2. Cook for 8 hours on low.
3. Serve warm.

Chicken Stroganoff

Time: 6 hrs. 15 mins.   Servings: 6
Ingredients:
2 shallots, chopped
2 cups sliced mushrooms
1 cup vegetable stock
1 tsp. dried Italian herbs
Salt and pepper
2 tbsp. butter
2 garlic cloves, chopped
3 chicken breasts, cubed
1 cup cream cheese
2 celery stalks, sliced
Cooked pasta of your choice for serving

Directions:
1. Heat the butter in a pan and add the chicken. Cook until golden then place in the crock pot.
2. Add the remaining ingredients and sprinkle with salt and pepper.
3. Cook for 6 hours on low.
4. Serve warm.

Creamy Chicken Stew

Time: 6 hrs. 15 mins.   Servings: 6
Ingredients:
2 potatoes, peeled and cubed
1 cup vegetable stock
1 shallot, sliced
2 tbsp. olive oil
Salt and pepper
1-can condensed cream of chicken soup
3 chicken breasts, cubed
1/2 head cauliflower, cut into florets
1 celery stalk, sliced

Directions:
1. Heat the oil in a frying pan and add the chicken. Cook for a few minutes, until it turns golden.
2. Transfer the chicken to your crock pot.
3. Add the remaining ingredients and sprinkle with salt and pepper.
4. Cook the stew for 6 hours on low.
5. Serve warm.

Pulled Chicken

Time: 8 hrs. 15 mins.   Servings: 8
Ingredients:
1 tsp. grated ginger
1 cup BBQ sauce
2 large sweet onions, sliced
4 chicken breasts
1 cup apple cider
Salt and pepper

Directions:
1. Put all the ingredients in your crock pot. Add salt and pepper to taste.
2. Cook for 8 hours on low.
3. When done, shred the chicken into fine threads using two forks.
4. Serve warm.

Sweet Glazed Chicken Drumsticks

Time: 5 hrs. 15 mins.   Servings: 4
Ingredients:
2-lbs. chicken drumsticks
2 green onions, chopped
1 cup pineapple juice
1/4 cup chicken stock
2 tbsp. soy sauce
2 tbsp. brown sugar
1 tsp. grated ginger
1/4 tsp. chili powder
White rice for serving

Directions:
1. Put the brown sugar, chili, pineapple juice, soy sauce, drumsticks, ginger, stock, and green onions in the crock pot.
2. Add salt and pepper to taste and cook for 5 hours on low.
3. Serve warm over rice.

Thai Chicken Vegetable Medley

Time: 4 hrs. 15 mins.   Servings: 6
Ingredients:
2 cups button mushrooms
4 garlic cloves, minced
1 leek, sliced
1 tbsp. red Thai curry paste
Salt and pepper
1/2 cup vegetable stock
2 zucchinis, sliced
2 red bell peppers, cored and sliced
2 chicken breasts, cut into strips
2 heirloom tomatoes, peeled and diced
1 cup coconut milk.

Directions:
1. Put all the ingredients in your crock pot. Add salt and pepper and cover.
2. Cook for 4 hours on low.
3. Serve the dish hot or cold.

Chicken Cordon Bleu

Time: 6 hrs. 15 mins.   Servings: 4
Ingredients:
4 chicken breasts, boneless and skinless
4 thick slices ham
4 slices cheddar cheese
1/2 cup vegetable stock
Salt and pepper to taste
1 tsp. dried thyme

Directions:
1. Add salt, pepper, and thyme to the chicken and place it in your crock pot.
2. Add a slice of ham and cheese and pour the stock in.
3. Cook for 6 hours on low.
4. Serve warm.

Hoisin Chicken

Time: 2 hrs. 30 mins.   Servings: 6
Ingredients:
3 chicken breasts, sliced.
1 tsp. sesame oil
1 tbsp. soy sauce
1/4 cup hoisin sauce
2 garlic cloves, minced
2 green onions, chopped
2 carrots, sliced
2 tbsp. sesame seeds
1/4 cup chicken stock

Directions:
1. Put the hoisin sauce, soy sauce, carrots, chicken stock, chicken, sesame oil, sesame seeds, and garlic in your crock pot.
2. Cover and cook for 2 hours 25 minutes on high.
3. Serve the chicken warm, topped with green onions.

Mango Chicken Sauté

Time: 2 hrs. 45 mins.   Servings: 6
Ingredients:
1-can fire roasted tomatoes
1/4 tsp. grated ginger
Salt and pepper to taste
1 cup chicken stock
1 chipotle pepper, chopped
4 garlic cloves, chopped
2 tbsp. canola oil
1/2 tsp. cumin powder
1 large sweet onion, sliced
2 chicken breasts, cut into thin strips
1 large mango, peeled and cubed

Directions:
1. Heat the canola oil in your crock pot and add the chicken. Cook for a few minutes until golden brown.
2. Place the chicken in your crock pot. Add the remaining ingredients and cover.
3. Cook for 2½ hours on high. Serve warm.

Spicy Hot Chicken Thighs

Time: 8 hrs. 15 mins.   Servings: 8
Ingredients:
1/2 tsp. garlic powder
1/2 tsp. cumin powder
Salt and pepper to taste
1/2 cup vegetable stock
1/4 cup hot sauce
8 chicken thighs
1/2 cup tomato sauce
2 tbsp. butter

Directions:
1. Mix the chicken thighs with the remaining ingredients, including salt and pepper, in the crock pot.
2. Cover and cook for 8 hours on low.
3. Serve warm.

Chicken Ravioli in Tomato Sauce

Time: 2 hrs. 45 mins.   Servings: 6
Ingredients:
Salt and pepper to taste
16 oz. chicken ravioli
1 pinch cumin powder
2 cups fresh spinach, shredded
1-can fire roasted tomatoes
1 cup vegetables stock
1 shallot, chopped
4 garlic cloves, minced
1/4 tsp. coriander powder

Directions:
1. Put the garlic, coriander powder, tomatoes, ravioli, shallot, stock, cumin and spinach in your slow cooker.
2. Add salt and pepper and cook for 2½ hours on high.
3. Serve the dish warm and fresh.

Creamy Chicken and Mushroom Pot Pie

Time: 6 hrs. 15 mins.   Servings: 6
Ingredients:
1/2 tsp. dried thyme
1 sheet puff pastry
1 cup frozen peas
1 cup vegetable stock
4 cups sliced cremini mushrooms
2 chicken breasts, cubed
1 large onion, chopped
4 carrots, sliced
Salt and pepper to taste

Directions:
1. Put the chicken, onion, peas, mushrooms, carrots, stock, and thyme in your crock pot.
2. Add salt and pepper, then top with the puff pastry.
3. Cover and cook for 6 hours on low.
4. Serve the pot pie warm.

Lemon Garlic Roasted Chicken

Time: 6 hrs. 15 mins.   Servings: 6
Ingredients:
1 lemon, sliced
1 thyme sprig
1 rosemary sprig
6 chicken thighs
6 garlic cloves, chopped
1/2 cup chicken stock
2 tbsp. butter

Directions:
1. Place the chicken in the crock pot, then add salt and pepper to taste.
2. Top the chicken with stock, thyme sprig, lemon slices, garlic, butter, and rosemary sprig.
3. Cook for 6 hours on low.
4. Serve the chicken warm.

Tarragon Chicken

Time: 6 hrs. 15 mins.   Servings: 6
Ingredients:
4 garlic cloves, minced
1 tsp. lemon zest
Salt and pepper
2 tbsp. chopped parsley for serving
1 tbsp. cornstarch
3-lbs. chicken drumsticks
1/2 cup heavy cream
1/2 cup chicken stock
2 tbsp. Dijon mustard
1 tsp. dried tarragon

Directions:
1. Put the cream, cornstarch, chicken stock, garlic, chicken, mustard, tarragon, and lemon zest in the crock pot.
2. Add salt and pepper and cook for 6 hours on low.
3. Serve the chicken warm and fresh.

Italian Fennel Braised Chicken

Time: 6 hrs. 30 mins.   Servings: 8
Ingredients:
1 tsp. dried basil
1 large fennel bulb, sliced
1 large onion, sliced
Salt and pepper to taste
1 rosemary sprig
1 cup chicken stock
2 garlic cloves, chopped
8 chicken thighs
1-can (15 oz.) cannellini beans, drained
2 yellow bell peppers, cored and sliced
2 ripe tomatoes, peeled and diced

Directions:
1. Mix the chicken, fennel and the remaining ingredients in the crock pot.
2. Add salt and pepper and cook for 6 hours on low.
3. Serve the chicken warm.

Swiss Cheese Saucy Chicken

Time: 3 hrs. 15 mins.   Servings: 4
Ingredients:
Salt and pepper
1/2 cup chicken stock
1 cup grated Swiss cheese
1 celery stalk, sliced.
4 boneless chicken breasts
1-can cream of mushrooms soup
1 shallot, sliced.

Directions:
1. Season the chicken with salt and pepper to taste.
2. Place the chicken in a crock pot and add the remaining ingredients.
3. Cook for 3 hours on high.
4. Serve the chicken warm with your favorite side dish.

Button Mushroom Chicken Stew

Time: 6 hrs. 15 mins.   Servings: 6
Ingredients:
1 cup vegetable stock
1 thyme sprig
2 tbsp. canola oil
Salt and pepper
2 garlic cloves, minced
1 shallot, chopped
2 chicken breasts, cubed
4 cups button mushrooms
1 cup cream cheese

Directions:
1. Heat the oil in a pan and add the chicken. Cook for about 5 minutes on medium heat, until it turns golden brown.
2. Transfer in the slow cooker and add the remaining ingredients.
3. Add salt and pepper to taste and cook for 6 hours on low.
4. Serve warm.

Red Salsa Chicken

Time: 8 hrs. 15 mins.   Servings: 8
Ingredients:
2 cups red salsa
Salt and pepper
1/2 cup chicken stock
8 chicken thighs
1 cup grated cheddar cheese

Directions:
1. Mix the chicken with the salsa and stock in the slow cooker.
2. Add the cheese and cook for 8 hours on low.
3. Serve the chicken warm.

Caramelized Onions Chicken Stew

Time: 6 hrs. 30 mins.   Servings: 6
Ingredients:
1 celery stalk, sliced
2 tbsp. canola oil
2 red bell peppers, cored and sliced
1/4 cup dry white wine
1-can fire roasted tomatoes
1/2 tsp. dried thyme
2 chicken breasts, cubed
3 large onions, sliced
4 bacon slices, chopped
Salt and pepper

Directions:
1. Heat the oil in a pan and add the bacon. Cook until crisp, then add the onions.
2. Cook for 10 minutes, until onions are soft.
3. Place in your slow cooker. Add the remaining ingredients and sprinkle with salt and pepper.
4. Cook for 6 hours on low.
5. Serve the stew warm.

Mexican Chicken Stew

Time: 8 hrs. 15 mins.   Servings: 8
Ingredients:
1 tsp. taco seasoning
1/2 tsp. chili powder
Salt and pepper
1 cup chicken stock
1 can (15 oz.) diced tomatoes
1 cup red salsa
1/2 cup cream cheese
4 chicken breasts, cubed.
1 can (15 oz.) black beans, drained
1 can (10 oz.) sweet corn, drained

Directions:
1. Put the chicken, beans, corn, tomatoes, red salsa, taco seasoning, chili powder, stock, and cream cheese in the slow cooker.
2. Add salt and pepper to taste and cook on low for 8 hours.
3. Serve the stew warm.

Whole Orange Glazed Chicken

Time: 2 hrs. 45 mins.   Servings: 4
Ingredients:
4 chicken thighs
1/2 cup chicken stock
1 large orange, cut into segments
2 tbsp. soy sauce
1 tbsp. honey
1 tsp. hot sauce
1/2 tsp. sesame seeds
Cooked white rice for serving

Directions:
1. Put all the ingredients in your crock pot.
2. Cover and cook for 2½ hours on high.
3. Serve the chicken warm over rice.

Chicken Cacciatore

Time: 7 hrs. 15 mins.   Servings: 8

Ingredients:

1 large onion, sliced
1/4 cup dry white wine
1 bay leaf
2 cups sliced mushrooms
2 tbsp. tomato paste
1 tbsp. cornstarch
1 tsp. dried basil
2-lbs. chicken drumsticks
1 red bell pepper, cored and sliced
1 yellow bell pepper, cored and sliced

2 garlic cloves, minced
1 cup chicken stock
2 celery stalks, sliced
2 carrots, sliced
2 tbsp. canola oil
1/2 tsp. dried oregano
Salt and pepper

Directions:

1. Heat the canola oil in a pan. Add the chicken and cook until golden.
2. Place the chicken in the crock pot and add the remaining ingredients.
3. Sprinkle with salt and pepper and cook for 7 hours on low.
4. Serve warm.

Arroz con Pollo

Time: 6 hrs. 15 mins.   Servings: 8

Ingredients:

1 cup green peas
1 cup sliced mushrooms
4 chicken breasts, halved
1 rosemary sprig
1 onion, chopped
Salt and pepper to taste
2 ripe tomatoes, peeled and diced

1 cup wild rice
2 cups vegetable stock
1 thyme sprig
2 celery stalks, sliced
1 red chili, chopped

Directions:

1. Put the onion, red chili, rice, green peas, celery, tomatoes, mushrooms, stock, and chicken in the crock pot.
2. Add the rosemary, thyme, salt, and pepper and cook for 6 hours on low.
3. Serve the dish warm.

Honey Sesame Glazed Chicken

Time: 6 hrs. 15 mins.   Servings: 4

Ingredients:

2 garlic cloves, minced
2 tbsp. soy sauce
1/2 tsp. red pepper flakes
1 tsp. grated ginger
1 tsp. sesame oil
2 tbsp. sesame seeds
4 chicken breasts
1/4 cup chicken stock
1/4 cup ketchup
3 tbsp. honey

Directions:

1. Put all ingredients in the crock pot.
2. Cover and for 6 hours cook on low.
3. Serve the chicken warm.

Honey Glazed Chicken Drumsticks

Time: 6 hrs. 15 mins.   Servings: 6

Ingredients:

2-lbs. chicken drumsticks
2 garlic cloves, minced
1/4 cup chicken stock
1/4 cup fresh orange juice
2 tbsp. soy sauce
1 tbsp. grated zest
2 tbsp. sesame seeds
1/4 tsp. chili powder
1 tsp. rice vinegar

Directions:

1. Put all ingredients in your crock pot.
2. Cover and cook for 6 hours on low.
3. Serve the chicken warm.

CHAPTER 3
SOUP RECIPES

Butternut Squash Creamy Soup

Time: 4 hrs. 15 mins   **Servings: 6**

Ingredients:

1 sweet onion, chopped
1 potato, peeled and cubed
3 cups water
1 pinch cayenne pepper
2 tablespoons olive oil
2 garlic cloves, chopped
2 cups butternut squash cubed
1 celery root, peeled and cubed

2 parsnips, cubed
Salt and pepper
2 cups chicken stock
1/4 teaspoon cumin powder

Directions:

1. Heat the oil in a pan and add the onion and garlic. Cook for 2-3 minutes, until softened, then place it in the slow cooker.
2. Add the remaining ingredients and salt and pepper to taste.
3. Cook the soup for 4 hours on low.
4. When done, remove the cover and purée the soup with an immersion blender.
5. Serve warm.

Creamy White Bean Soup

Time: 4 hrs. 15 mins   **Servings: 6**

Ingredients:

2 garlic cloves, chopped
2 cups chicken stock
1/2 teaspoon dried thyme
1 tablespoon olive oil
1/2 celery root, peeled and cubed
1 sweet onion, chopped
1 can (15 oz.) white beans, drained

1 parsnip, diced
3 cups water
Salt and pepper

Directions:

1. Heat the oil in a pan and add the onion, garlic, celery, and parsnip. Cook for 5 minutes, until softened, then put the mixture in the slow cooker.
2. Add the remaining necessary ingredients and cook for 4 hours on low.
3. When done, purée the soup with an immersion blender and blend until smooth and creamy.
4. Serve warm.

Creamy Bacon Soup

Time: 1 hr. 45 mins   **Servings: 6**

Ingredients:

1 tablespoon olive oil
1 sweet onion, chopped
1/2 celery root, cubed
3 cups water
1 1/2 pounds potatoes, peeled and cubed

6 bacon slices, chopped
1 parsnip, diced
2 cups chicken stock
Salt and pepper

Directions:

1. Heat the oil in a pan, then add the bacon. Cook until soft, then transfer the bacon to a plate.
2. Pour the bacon fat in the slow cooker and add the remaining ingredients.
3. Add salt and pepper and cook for 1 1/2 hours on high.
4. When done, blend the soup with an immersion blender until smooth.
5. Pour the mixture into a bowl and top with bacon.
6. Serve right away.

Pinto Bean Chili Soup

Time: 4 hrs. 15 mins   **Servings: 10**

Ingredients:

2 tablespoons olive oil
1 garlic clove, chopped
1/2 teaspoon chili powder
1/2 teaspoon cumin powder
2 cups butternut squash cubes
2 cups cooked pinto beans
1/2 cup canned sweet corn, drained
2 tablespoons tomato paste
2 red bell peppers, cored and diced

1 red onion, chopped
4 cups chicken stock
1 bay leaf
1 thyme sprig
2 cups water

Directions:

1. Heat the oil in a pan and add the onion. Cook for 2 minutes, until softened.
2. Put the onion in your slow cooker. Add all remaining ingredients.
3. Add salt and pepper to taste, then cook the soup for 4 hours on low.
4. Serve hot or cold.

Black Bean Soup

Time: 7 hrs. 15 mins   **Servings: 8**
Ingredients:

1/2 pound black beans, rinsed
1 parsnip, diced
1 red bell peppers, cored and diced
1/2 cup sour cream for serving
2 tablespoons tomato paste
1/2 teaspoon cumin powder
1/4 teaspoon chili powder
1 sweet onion, chopped
2 tablespoons chopped cilantro for serving

Salt and pepper
1 celery stalk, diced
5 cups water
2 tomatoes, diced
1 bay leaf
2 carrots, diced
2 cups chicken stock

Directions:
1. Put the chicken stock, water, black beans, and vegetables in your slow cooker.
2. Add the bay leaf, salt, cumin powder, chili powder, and pepper and cook the soup for 7 hours on low.
3. When done, add the cilantro. Pour the soup in bowls, top with sour cream, and then serve.

Posole Soup

Time: 6 hrs. 15 mins   **Servings: 8**
Ingredients:

1 pound pork tenderloin, cubed
1 sweet onion, chopped
1/2 teaspoon cumin powder
1/2 teaspoon dried oregano
1/4 teaspoon chili powder
1 can sweet corn, drained
2 jalapeno peppers, chopped
Salt and pepper to taste
1 can (15 oz.) black beans, drained

2 garlic cloves, chopped
2 cups water
1/2 teaspoon dried basil
1 tablespoons canola oil
1 cup diced tomatoes
4 cups chicken stock
2 limes, juiced

Directions:
1. Heat the canola oil in a pan and add the tenderloin. Cook for 5 minutes.
2. Add the pork to the slow cooker and add the remaining ingredients, except the lime juice.
3. Add salt and pepper and cook for 6 hours on low.
4. When done, add the lime juice and serve warm.

Three Bean Soup

Time: 4 hrs. 30 mins   **Servings: 10**
Ingredients:

2 tablespoons olive oil
2 garlic cloves, minced
2 cups chicken stock
1 cup diced tomatoes
1 lime, juiced
2 tablespoons chopped parsley
2 red bell peppers, cored and diced
1 can (15 oz.) black beans, drained
1 can (15 oz.) kidney beans, drained
1 can (15 oz.) pinto beans, drained

2 sweet onions, chopped
2 carrots, diced
4 cups water
Salt and pepper
1/2 cup sour cream

Directions:
1. Heat the oil in a pan and add the garlic, peppers, onions, and carrot. Cook for 5 minutes.
2. Put the mixture in the slow cooker and add the tomatoes, beans, stock, water, and salt & pepper.
3. Cook for 4 hours on low.
4. When done, add the lime juice.
5. Pour the soup into serving bowls and add sour cream and parsley.
6. Serve warm.

Provencal Beef Soup

Time: 7 hrs. 15 mins   **Servings: 8**
Ingredients:

Salt and pepper
1 sweet onion, chopped
1 can diced tomatoes
1 cup beef stock
1 cup red wine
1 garlic clove, chopped
2 carrots, sliced
2 tablespoons olive oil
1 pound beef roast, cubed
1 celery stalk, sliced
4 cups water
1/2 teaspoon dried thyme
1 bay leaf

Directions:
1. Heat the oil in a pan and add the beef roast. Cook for a few minutes, then put the beef in a slow cooker.
2. Add the remaining ingredients and salt and pepper to taste.
3. Cook for 7 hours on low.
4. Serve warm.

Sausage Bean Soup

Time: 3 hrs. 15 mins   **Servings: 8**
Ingredients:

2 bacon slices, chopped
1 garlic clove, chopped
1/2 teaspoon dried rosemary
4 pork sausages, sliced
1 parsnip, diced
2 cups chicken stock
1/2 teaspoon dried thyme
1 can (15 oz.) white beans, drained

1 sweet onion, chopped
1 can diced tomatoes
4 cups water
1 carrot, diced
1 celery stalk, sliced
Salt and pepper

Directions:
1. Place a pan over medium heat and add the bacon. Sauté for 2-3 minutes until crisp.
2. Place the bacon in your slow cooker.
3. Add the remaining ingredients and salt and pepper to taste.
4. Cook the soup for 3 hours on high.
5. Serve warm.

Curried Lentil Soup

Time: 4 hrs. 15 mins   **Servings: 8**
Ingredients:

1 teaspoon curry powder
1/4 teaspoon ground ginger
Salt and pepper
1 cup dried lentils, rinsed
1 carrot, diced
1 celery stalk, sliced
1 parsnip, diced
1 cup diced tomatoes
4 bacon slices, chopped
1 sweet onion, chopped
2 garlic cloves, chopped
2 cups chicken stock
4 cups water
1 lime, juiced
2 tablespoons chopped parsley

Directions:
1. Place a pan over medium heat and add the bacon. Cook for a few minutes until crisp.
2. Place the bacon in a slow cooker and add the lentils, carrot, water, curry powder, celery, onion, garlic, parsnip, tomatoes, stock, and ginger.
3. Add salt and pepper; cook for 4 hours on low.
4. When done, add the lime juice and chopped parsley and serve warm.

Tuscan Chicken Soup

Time: 6 hrs. 15 mins   **Servings: 6**
Ingredients:

2 chicken breasts, cubed
1 shallot, chopped
1 parsnip, diced
1 can diced tomatoes
2 cups water
1 teaspoon dried Italian herbs
1 red bell peppers, cored and diced
1 can (15 oz.) cannellini beans, drained

2 tablespoons canola oil
1 carrot, diced
1 celery stalk, sliced
2 cups chicken stock
Salt and pepper
2 oz. Parmesan shavings

Directions:
1. Heat the canola oil in a pan and add the chicken. Cook for a few minutes until golden brown.
2. Transfer the chicken to your slow cooker.
3. Add the shallot, parsnip, beans, tomatoes, stock, celery, bell peppers, and water.
4. Add salt, pepper, and herbs; cook for 6 hours on low.
5. Serve warm, topped with Parmesan.

Tomato Beef Soup

Time: 8 hrs. 15 mins   **Servings: 8**
Ingredients:

2 tablespoons olive oil
2 bacon slices, chopped
2 pounds beef roast, cubed
2 sweet onions, chopped
2 tomatoes, peeled and diced
2 cups tomato sauce
1 cup beef stock
3 cups water
Salt and pepper
1 thyme sprig
1 rosemary sprig

Directions:
1. Heat the oil in a pan and add the bacon. Cook until crisp and add the beef roast. Cook for 5 minutes.
2. Transfer the beet and bacon in a slow cooker.
3. Add the remaining ingredients and also salt and pepper.
4. Cook for 8 hours on low.
5. Serve warm.

Coconut Squash Soup

Time: 2 hrs. 15 mins   **Servings: 6**
Ingredients:

1 tablespoon olive oil
1/2 teaspoon grated ginger
3 cups butternut squash cubes
2 cups water
1 tablespoon tomato paste
1 tablespoon curry paste
1 teaspoon Worcestershire sauce

1 shallot, chopped
2 garlic cloves, minced
2 cups chicken stock
1 cup coconut milk
Salt and pepper
1 teaspoon brown sugar

Directions:

1. Heat the oil in a pan and add the shallot, ginger, garlic, and curry paste. Cook for 1 minute. Place the mixture in a slow cooker.
2. Add the remaining ingredients and also salt and pepper.
3. Cover and cook for 2 hours on high.
4. When done, blend the soup with an immersion blender until smooth.
5. Serve warm.

Creamy Potato Soup

Time: 6 hrs. 15 mins   **Servings: 6**
Ingredients:

6 bacon slices, chopped
1 sweet onion, chopped
1 can condensed chicken soup
6 medium size potatoes, peeled and cubed
2 cups water
Salt and pepper to taste
1 1/2 cups half and half
1 tablespoon chopped parsley

Directions:

1. Place a pan over medium heat and add the bacon. Cook until soft, then transfer the bacon and its fat to a slow cooker.
2. Add the chicken soup, potatoes, onion, water, salt and pepper and cook for 4 hours on low.
3. Add the half and half and continue cooking for another 2 hours.
4. When done, add the chopped parsley and serve warm.

Italian Wedding Soup

Time: 6 hrs. 15 mins   **Servings: 6**
Ingredients:

1/2 teaspoon dried thyme
1 carrot, sliced
1 pound beef roast, cubed
1 large sweet onion, chopped
1/2 cup uncooked barley
1/2 teaspoon dried oregano
2 ripe tomatoes, peeled and diced

Salt and pepper
1 parsnip, sliced
2 tablespoons olive oil
3 cups water
2 cups beef stock
1 teaspoon dried basil

Directions:

1. Heat the oil in a pan and add the beef. Cook for 5-6 minutes.
2. Put the beef in a slow cooker and add the remaining ingredients.
3. Add salt and pepper and cook the soup for 6 hours on low.
4. Serve warm.

Quick Lentil and Ham Soup

Time: 1 hr. 45 mins   **Servings: 6**
Ingredients:

1 tablespoon olive oil
1/2 cup tomato sauce
1 1/2 cups chicken stock
Salt and pepper to taste
4 oz. ham, diced
1 shallot, chopped
1/2 teaspoon dried oregano
1/2 teaspoon dried basil
1 carrot, diced
1 celery stalk, sliced
1 cup dried lentils, rinsed
2 cups water

Directions:

1. Mix oregano, basil, olive oil, water, tomato sauce, celery, lentils, ham, carrot, shallot, and stock.
2. Add salt and pepper and cook for 1 1/2 hours on high.
3. Serve the soup hot or cold.

Split Pea Sausage Soup

Time: 6 hrs. 15 mins   **Servings: 8**

Ingredients:
2 carrots, diced
2 tablespoons tomato paste
Salt and pepper to taste
1 lemon, juiced
1 celery stalk, diced
1 garlic clove, chopped
2 cups split peas, rinsed
8 cups water
4 Italian sausages, sliced
1 sweet onion, chopped
1 red chili, chopped
1/2 teaspoon dried oregano
2 tablespoons chopped parsley

Directions:
1. Put the celery, garlic, red chili, split peas, onion, carrots, water, sausages, oregano and tomato paste in your slow cooker.
2. Add salt and pepper and cook for 6 hours on low.
3. When done, add the lemon juice and parsley
4. Serve warm.

Zucchini Soup

Time: 2 hrs. 15 mins   **Servings: 6**

Ingredients:
1 pound Italian sausage, sliced
2 celery stalks, sliced
2 zucchinis, cubed
2 large potatoes, peeled and cubed
2 yellow bell peppers, cored and diced
2 carrots, sliced
1 shallot, chopped
3 cups water
2 cups vegetable stock
1/2 teaspoon dried oregano
1/2 teaspoon dried basil
1/4 teaspoon garlic powder
Salt and pepper to taste
2 tablespoons chopped parsley

Directions:
1. Put the zucchini, potatoes, sausages, celery stalks, shallot, water, bell peppers, carrots, stock, and seasoning in your slow cooker.
2. Add salt and pepper and cook for 2 hours on high.
3. When done, add the parsley and serve warm.

Beef Taco Soup

Time: 7 hrs. 15 mins   **Servings: 8**

Ingredients:
1 pound beef stock, cubed
1 garlic clove, chopped
1 cup canned corn, drained
2 tablespoons taco seasoning
1 jalapeno pepper, chopped
3 cups water
1 avocado, sliced
1 tablespoon olive oil
1 onion, chopped
1 cup tomato sauce
1 cup dark beer
Salt and pepper
2 cups beef stock
1/2 cup sour cream

1 can (15 oz.) black beans, drained
1 can (15 oz.) cannellini beans, drained

Directions:

1. Heat the oil in a pan and add the onion, beef, and garlic. Cook for 2 minutes then place in a slow cooker.
2. Add the tomato sauce, beer, beans, corn, taco seasoning, and jalapeno.
3. Add salt and pepper and cook for 7 hours on low.
4. Pour the soup into serving bowls and to with a dollop of sour cream and avocado slices.

Spicy Black Bean Soup

Time: 6 hrs. 15 mins   **Servings: 6**

Ingredients:
1/2 cup diced tomatoes
Salt and pepper
2 jalapeno peppers, chopped
2 cups chicken stock
1 can (15 oz.) black beans, drained
1/2 teaspoon cumin powder
1/2 cup sour cream
4 cups water
1 tablespoon olive oil
1 shallot, chopped
1 carrot, diced
1/2 teaspoon chili powder

Directions:
1. Put the carrot, jalapeno peppers, olive oil, shallot, stock, beans, water, and spices in a slow cooker.
2. Add salt and pepper and cook for 6 hours on low.
3. Serve warm, topped with sour cream.

Chicken Sausage Soup

Time: 6 hrs. 30 mins　　　　**Servings: 8**

Ingredients:

1 sweet onion, chopped
2 garlic cloves, chopped
1/2 teaspoon dried basil
1/4 cup dry white wine
1/2 cup short pasta
2 tablespoons chopped parsley
1 red bell pepper, cored and diced
1/2 teaspoon dried oregano
1 pound Italian sausages, sliced

1 carrot, diced
1 can cannellini beans
1 can diced tomatoes
2 cups chicken stock
Salt and pepper
3 cups water

Directions:

1. Put the oregano, basil, tomatoes, garlic, bell pepper, sausages, onion, carrot, beans, wine, stock and water in a slow cooker.
2. Cook for 1 hour on high then add the pasta and continue cooking for another 5 hours.
3. Serve warm with freshly chopped parsley.

Beef Cabbage Soup

Time: 7 hrs. 30 mins　　　　**Servings: 8**

Ingredients:

1/2 teaspoon cumin seeds
Salt and pepper to taste
1 sweet onion, chopped
1 carrot, grated
1 small cabbage head, shredded
1 pound beef roast, cubed
2 tablespoons olive oil
1 can (15 oz.) diced tomatoes
2 cups beef stock
2 cups water

Directions:

1. Heat the oil in a pan and add the beef roast. Cook for 5-6 minutes then transfer the meat to a slow cooker.
2. Add the remaining ingredients.
3. Cook for 7 hours on low.
4. Serve warm.

Vegetable Beef Soup

Time: 7 hrs. 15 mins　　　　**Servings: 8**

Ingredients:

1 carrot, sliced
1 garlic clove, chopped
1/2 head cauliflower, cut into florets
4 cups water
Salt and pepper
1 pound beef roast, cubed
2 large potatoes, peeled and cubed
1 cup diced tomatoes
1/2 teaspoon dried basil
2 cups beef stock
2 tablespoons canola oil
1 celery stalk, sliced
1 sweet onion, chopped

Directions:

1. Heat the oil in a pan and add the beef. Cook for a few minutes then place the beef in a slow cooker.
2. Add the remaining ingredients and also salt and pepper.
3. Cover and cook for 7 hours on low.
4. Serve it warm.

Sweet Corn Chowder

Time: 6 hrs. 15 mins　　　　**Servings: 8**

Ingredients:

2 shallots, chopped
2 cups chicken stock
2 cups water
Salt and pepper
1 can (15 oz.) sweet corn, drained
4 medium size potatoes, peeled and cubed
1 celery stalk, sliced

Directions

1. Put the celery, corn, shallot, potatoes, stock, and water in a slow cooker.
2. Add salt and pepper and cook for 6 hours on low.
3. When done, remove a few tablespoons of corn from the pot then purée the rest of the soup in the pot.
4. Pour the soup into serving bowls and add the reserved corn.
5. Serve warm.

Chicken Enchilada Soup

Time: 6 hrs. 30 mins   **Servings: 8**

Ingredients:

1 bay leaf
Salt and pepper to taste
2 garlic cloves, chopped
1 chicken breast, diced
1 can (15 oz.) diced tomatoes
1 tablespoon olive oil
2 shallots, chopped
4 cups water
1/2 teaspoon cumin powder
1/2 teaspoon chili powder
1 can (15 oz.) sweet corn, drained
1 can (4 oz.) green chile, chopped
2 cups chicken stock

Directions:

1. Put the garlic, olive oil, shallots, and chicken in a pan and cook for 5 minutes.
2. Put the chicken in your slow cooker and add the remaining ingredients.
3. Add salt and pepper and cook for 6 hours on low.
4. Serve warm.

Italian Barley Soup

Time: 6 hrs. 15 mins   **Servings: 8**

Ingredients:

2 tablespoons olive oil
1 garlic clove, chopped
1 celery stalk, diced
2 cups vegetable stock
1 teaspoon dried oregano
1 lemon, juiced
2 red bell peppers, cored and diced
2 tomatoes, peeled and diced
2 cups fresh spinach, chopped

1 shallot, chopped
1 carrot, diced
3 cups water
2/3 cup pearl barley
1 teaspoon dried basil
Salt and pepper

Directions:

1. Heat the oil in a pan and add the shallot, garlic, carrot and celery, and also bell peppers.
2. Cook for 5 minutes just until softened then place in a slow cooker.
3. Add the remaining ingredients and also salt and pepper.
4. Cook for 6 hours on low.
5. Serve warm.

Ham Bone Cabbage Soup

Time: 7 hrs. 15 mins   **Servings: 8**

Ingredients:

1 mediums size cabbage head, shredded
2 tablespoons tomato paste
1 can diced tomatoes
1 thyme sprig
1 lemon, juiced
1 ham bone
1 sweet onion, chopped
2 cups beef stock
Salt and pepper to taste
1 bay leaf

Directions:

1. Put the stock, bay leaf, cabbage, tomato paste, ham bone, onion, tomatoes, and thyme sprig in your slow cooker.
2. Add salt and pepper and cook for 7 hours on low.
3. When done, add the lemon juice
4. Serve warm.

Lima Bean Soup

Time: 7 hrs. 15 mins   **Servings: 8**

Ingredients:

2 carrots, diced
2 potatoes, peeled and cubed
1 celery stalk, sliced
2 bacon slices, chopped
4 cups frozen lima beans
3 cups water
1 bay leaf
2 shallots, chopped
Salt and pepper
1 can diced tomatoes
2 cups vegetable stock
1 tablespoon chopped cilantro

Directions:

1. Put the shallots, potatoes, celery, carrots, bacon, lima beans, and tomatoes in a slow cooker.
2. Add the remaining necessary ingredients, except cilantro and sprinkle with salt and pepper.
3. Cook for 7 hours on low.
4. When done, add the chopped cilantro.
5. Serve warm.

Okra Vegetable Soup

Time: 7 hrs. 15 mins   **Servings: 8**

Ingredients:
1 pound ground beef
2 tablespoons canola oil
2 shallots, chopped
1 carrot, sliced
1 can fire roasted tomatoes, chopped
2 cups chopped okra
1/2 cup green peas
2 potatoes, peeled and cubed
1/2 cup sweet corn, drained
Salt and pepper to taste
2 cups water
2 cups chicken stock
1 lemon, juiced

Directions:
1. Heat the oil in a pan and add the beef. Cook for a few minutes then place the meat in a slow cooker.
2. Add the corn, water, tomatoes, okra, shallots, carrot, peas, potatoes, and stock, as well as lemon juice, salt, and pepper.
3. Cook the soup for 7 hours on low.
4. Serve warm.

Mexican Beef Soup

Time: 8 hrs. 15 mins   **Servings: 6**

Ingredients:
1/2 cup red salsa
1 chipotle pepper, chopped
Salt and pepper to taste
1 pound ground beef
1 sweet onion, chopped
2 cups beef stock
1 can (15 oz. diced tomatoes
2 tablespoons canola oil
2 red bell peppers, cored and diced
1 can (15 oz. black beans, drained
3 cups water

Directions:
1. Heat the oil in a pan and add the beef. Cook for 5 minutes, stirring often, then transfer the beef in your slow cooker.
2. Add the remaining ingredients and adjust the taste with salt and pepper.
3. Cook on low for 8 hours.
4. Serve warm or cold.

Hungarian Borscht

Time: 8 hrs. 15 mins   **Servings: 8**

Ingredients:
1 pound beef roast, cubed
2 potatoes, peeled and cubed
2 tablespoons tomato paste
4 cups water
1/2 teaspoon cumin seeds
1 teaspoon red wine vinegar
1 teaspoon honey
4 medium size beets, peeled and cubed
2 tablespoons canola oil
1 sweet onion, chopped
Salt and pepper
1 cup vegetable stock
1 can diced tomatoes
1 teaspoon dried parsley
1/2 teaspoon dried dill

Directions:
1. Heat the oil in a pan and add the beef. Cook for a few minutes until golden.
2. Place the meat in a slow cooker and add the potatoes, onion, beets, tomatoes, and tomato paste.
3. Add salt and pepper, as well as the remaining ingredients and cook on low for 8 hours.
4. Serve warm or cold

Chicken Rice Soup

Time: 7 hrs. 15 mins   **Servings: 8**

Ingredients:
2 tablespoons canola oil
2/3 cup white rice, rinsed
Salt and pepper
2 chicken breasts, cubed
2 carrots, diced
2 red bell peppers, cored and diced
1 can diced tomatoes
2 cups water
2 cups chicken stock
1 celery stalk, sliced
1 sweet onion, chopped
1 parsnip, diced

Directions:
1. Heat the canola oil in a pan and add the chicken. Cook for 5 minutes until golden.
2. Transfer the chicken to a slow cooker and add the remaining ingredients.
3. Add salt and pepper and cook for 7 hours on low.
4. Serve warm.

Ham and Potato Chowder

Time: 4 hrs. 15 mins   Servings: 8

Ingredients:

1 cup sweet corn, drained
1/2 teaspoon celery seeds
1 can condensed chicken soup
2 cups water
4 potatoes, peeled and cubed
1 sweet onion, chopped
1 tablespoon olive oil
Salt and pepper
1 cup diced ham
1/2 teaspoon cumin seeds

Directions:

1. Combine the chicken soup, onion, water, potatoes, olive oil, ham, and corn in a slow cooker.
2. Add the celery seeds and cumin seeds and sprinkle with salt and pepper.
3. Cook for 4 hours on high.
4. Serve warm.

Potato Kielbasa Soup

Time: 6 hrs. 15 mins   Servings: 8

Ingredients:

1 parsnip, diced
1 garlic clove, chopped
1 pound kielbasa sausages, sliced
1 sweet onion, chopped
2 carrots, diced
2 red bell peppers, cored and diced
2 large potatoes, peeled and cubed
Salt and pepper to taste
2 cups chicken stock
3 cups water
1/2 pound fresh spinach, shredded
1 lemon, juiced

Directions:

1. Combine the sausages, garlic, potatoes, onion, carrots, parsnip, and bell peppers in a slow cooker.
2. Add the spinach, stock, water, and lemon juice then add salt and pepper.
3. Cook for 6 hours on low.
4. Serve warm.

Curried Corn Chowder

Time: 8 hrs. 15 mins   Servings: 8

Ingredients:

1 can (15 oz. sweet corn, drained
1 1/2 cups whole milk
Salt and pepper
2 large potatoes, peeled and cubed
1 sweet onion, chopped
2 garlic cloves, chopped
2 cups chicken stock
1/2 chili pepper, chopped
1/4 teaspoon cumin seeds

Directions:

1. Mix the sweet corn, potatoes, onion, garlic, stock, and chili pepper in your slow cooker.
2. Add the remaining ingredients and sprinkle with salt and pepper.
3. Cook for 8 hours on low.
4. Serve warm.

Two-Fish Soup

Time: 6 hrs. 15 mins   Servings: 8

Ingredients:

3 salmon fillets, cubed
3 cod fillets, cubed
2 tablespoons chopped parsley
1 red bell pepper, cored and diced
1 chipotle pepper, chopped
1 carrot, diced
Salt and pepper
1 tablespoon canola oil
1 sweet onion, chopped
1 celery stalk, diced
1 cup diced tomatoes
1 lemon, juiced

Directions:

1. Heat the canola oil in a pan and add the onion. Cook for 2 minutes until softened.
2. Place the onion in a slow cooker and add the remaining ingredients.
3. Add salt and pepper and cook for 6 hours on low.
4. Serve warm.

Creamy Cauliflower Soup

Time: 3 hrs. 15 mins   Servings: 6

Ingredients:
Salt and pepper
1/2 cup water
1 head cauliflower, cut into florets
2 medium size potatoes, peeled and cubed
1 tablespoon canola oil
1 sweet onion, chopped
2 garlic cloves, chopped
1 can condensed cream of chicken soup
1/2 cup grated Parmesan cheese

Directions:
1. Heat the oil in a pan and add the onion. Cook for 2 minutes then transfer the onion in your slow cooker.
2. Add the remaining necessary ingredients, except the cheese, and season with salt and pepper.
3. Cook on high for 3 hours.
4. When done, purée with an immersion blender.
5. Serve warm.

Winter Veggie Soup

Time: 6 hrs. 30 mins   Servings: 8

Ingredients:
1 celery stalk, sliced
1/2 head cabbage, shredded
1 parsnip, sliced
1 sweet onion, chopped
2 carrots, sliced
1 celery root, peeled and cubed
Salt and pepper
1/4 cup white rice, rinsed
1 lemon, juiced
2 cups vegetable stock
3 cups water
1 cup diced tomatoes

Directions:
1. Add the onion, water, tomatoes, carrots, celery, cabbage, parsnip, celery, stock, and rice in your slow cooker.
2. Add salt and pepper and also the rice and cook for 6 hours on low.
3. Serve warm.

Spiced Creamy Pumpkin Soup

Time: 5 hrs. 15 mins   Servings: 6

Ingredients:
1 thyme sprig
1/2 cinnamon stick
2 cups chicken stock
1/2 teaspoon cumin powder
1/4 teaspoon chili powder
2 garlic cloves, chopped
1 medium sugar pumpkin, peeled and cubed
Salt and pepper
1 star anise
2 carrots, sliced
2 tablespoons olive oil
1 shallot, chopped
2 cups water

Directions:
1. Mix the carrots, garlic, shallot, and olive oil in a pan. Cook for 5 minutes until softened.
2. Place the mixture in a slow cooker and add the remaining ingredients, including the spices.
3. Cook for 5 hours on low then remove the thyme sprig, cinnamon, and star anise and purée with an immersion blender.
4. Serve warm.

Kielbasa Kale Soup

Time: 6 hrs. 15 mins   Servings: 8

Ingredients:
1 cup diced tomatoes
1 pound kielbasa sausages, sliced
1/2 pound kale, shredded
2 cups chicken stock
2 cups water
Salt and pepper
1 sweet onion, chopped
1 parsnip, diced
1 red bell pepper, cored and diced
1 can (15 oz.) white beans, drained
1 carrot, diced
1/2 teaspoon dried oregano
1/2 teaspoon dried basil

Directions:
1. Put the carrot, parsnip, kielbasa sausages, onion, bell pepper, white beans, tomatoes and kale in a slow cooker.
2. Add the remaining ingredients and also salt and pepper.
3. Cook for 6 hours on low.
4. Serve the soup hot or cold.

Lemony Salmon Soup

Time: 4 hrs. 15 mins   **Servings: 6**

Ingredients:

1 shallot, chopped
1 celery stalk, sliced
1 teaspoon lemon zest
1/2 teaspoon dried oregano
2 cups water
1 pound salmon fillets, cubed
1 red bell pepper, cored and diced
1/2 teaspoon dried basil

1 garlic clove, chopped
1 carrot, sliced
1 parsnip, sliced
2 cups milk
1 lemon, juiced
Salt and pepper

Directions:

1. Put the shallot, carrot, parsnip, garlic, celery, and bell pepper in a slow cooker.
2. Add the water, lemon juice, dried herbs, milk, and lemon zest and cook for 1 hour on high.
3. Add the fish and salt and pepper to taste.
4. Cook for 3 extra hours on low.
5. Serve the soup hot or cold.

Creamy Noodle Soup

Time: 8 hrs. 15 mins   **Servings: 8**

Ingredients:

2 shallots, chopped
1 celery stalk, sliced
1 cup green peas
6 oz. egg noodles
2 cups water
2 cups chicken stock
1 can condensed chicken soup
2 chicken breasts, cubed
2 tablespoons all-purpose flour
Salt and pepper

Directions:

1. Coat the chicken with salt, pepper and flour and place it in your slow cooker.
2. Add the remaining ingredients and sprinkle with salt and pepper.
3. Cover and cook for 8 hours on low.
4. Serve warm.

Asparagus Crab Soup

Time: 2 hrs. 15 mins   **Servings: 6**

Ingredients:

1 tablespoon olive oil
1 shallot, chopped
1 celery stalk, sliced
1 bunch asparagus, trimmed and chopped
1 cup green peas
1 cup chicken stock
2 cups water
Salt and pepper to taste
1 can crab meat, drained

Directions:

1. Heat the oil in a pan and add the shallot and celery. Cook for 2 minutes until softened then place in a slow cooker.
2. Add the green peas, stock, asparagus, and water and season with salt and pepper.
3. Cook for 2 hours. on high.
4. When done, purée the soup with an immersion blender until creamy.
5. Pour into serving bowls and top with crabmeat.

Chunky Potato Ham Soup

Time: 8 hrs. 15 mins   **Servings: 8**

Ingredients:

1 leek, sliced
2 cups chicken stock
3 cups water
Salt and pepper
1 celery stalk, sliced
2 carrots, sliced
2 cups diced ham
1 sweet onion, chopped
1 garlic clove, chopped
2 pounds potatoes, peeled and cubed
1/2 teaspoon dried oregano
1/2 teaspoon dried basil

Directions:

1. Put all the ingredients in a slow cooker.
2. Add salt and pepper and cook for 8 hours on low.
3. Serve the soup hot or cold.

Leek Potato Soup

Time: 6 hrs. 30 mins   **Servings: 8**
Ingredients:

4 leeks, sliced
4 bacon slices, chopped
2 cups chicken stock
1 bay leaf
1 thyme sprig
1/4 teaspoon cayenne pepper
1/4 teaspoon smoked paprika
4 large potatoes, peeled and cubed

1 tablespoon olive oil
1 celery stalk, sliced
3 cups water
Salt and pepper
1 rosemary sprig

Directions:

1. Heat the oil in a pan and add the bacon. Cook until crisp, then add the leeks.
2. Cook for 5 minutes until softened, then transfer to your slow cooker.
3. Add the remaining ingredients and cook for about 6 hours on low.
4. Serve warm.

Creamy Leek and Potato Soup

Time: 6 hrs. 15 mins   **Servings: 6**
Ingredients:

1 tablespoon all-purpose flour
Salt and pepper
1/2 cup heavy cream
2 cups chicken stock
2 tablespoons olive oil
2 leeks, sliced
2 cups water
4 large potatoes, peeled and cubed
1 thyme sprig

Directions:

1. Heat the oil in a pan and add the leeks. Cook for 5 minutes until softened. Add the flour and cook for another minute.
2. Place the mixture in a slow cooker and add the remaining ingredients, except the cream.
3. Cook for 6 hours on low.
4. When done, remove the thyme sprig, add the cream and purée the soup with an immersion blender.
5. Serve the soup hot or cold.

Minestrone Soup

Time: 6 hrs. 15 mins   **Servings: 8**
Ingredients:

2 cups water
2 carrots, diced
1 sweet onion, chopped
1 cup frozen green peas
1 teaspoon dried oregano
1 can red beans, drained
1 cup small pasta
2 tablespoons chopped parsley
4 ripe tomatoes, peeled and diced
2 tablespoons tomato paste
4 sun-dried tomatoes, chopped
Grated Parmesan for serving
2 garlic cloves, chopped

4 cups vegetable stock
2 celery stalks, diced
1 zucchini, cubed
1 thyme sprig
1 bay leaf
Salt and pepper

Directions:

1. Put the tomatoes, tomato paste and the remaining ingredients, except chopped parsley, in a slow cooker.
2. Add salt and pepper and cook the soup for 6 hours on low.
3. Serve warm and top with chopped parsley and grated Parmesan.

Roasted Bell Pepper Quinoa Soup

Time: 6 hrs. 30 mins   **Servings: 6**
Ingredients:

1 shallot, chopped
1 pinch cayenne pepper
Salt and pepper
1 garlic clove, chopped
4 roasted red bell peppers, chopped
1/2 cup red quinoa, rinsed
1/2 teaspoon dried oregano
1/2 teaspoon dried basil
1/2 cup tomato paste
2 cups vegetable stock
1 cup water

Directions:

1. Put the shallot, tomato paste, stock, garlic, bell peppers, and water in your slow cooker.
2. Add the quinoa, herbs and spices, and salt and pepper; cover.
3. Cook for 6 hours on low.
4. Serve warm.

Red Chili Quinoa Soup

Time: 3 hrs. 15 mins   Servings: 8
Ingredients:
Salt and pepper
1/2 teaspoon chili powder
1/2 celery root, peeled and diced
1 can diced tomatoes
1/2 cup quinoa, rinsed
2 shallots, chopped
Sour cream for serving
1 carrot, diced
1 can (15 oz.) red beans, drained
2 cups water
2 cups chicken stock
2 tablespoons chopped cilantro for serving.
Directions:
1. Put the carrot, celery, shallots, and diced tomatoes in your slow cooker.
2. Add the quinoa, water, stock, and chili powder and sprinkle with salt and pepper.
3. Cook for 3 hours on high.
4. Serve warm, topped with cilantro and sour cream.

Corn and Red Pepper Chowder

Time: 8 hrs. 15 mins   Servings: 8
Ingredients:
1/4 teaspoon smoked paprika
1/4 teaspoon cumin powder
2 cups water
Salt and pepper
2 tablespoons olive oil
2 large potatoes, peeled and cubed
2 cups frozen sweet corn
2 cups chicken stock
1 shallot, chopped
1 red bell pepper, cored and diced

Directions:
1. Heat the oil in a pan and stir in the shallot. Cook until softened then place in your slow cooker.
2. Add the remaining ingredients and also salt and pepper.
3. Cook for 8 hours on low.
4. When done, purée the soup in a blender
5. Serve it warm.

Chunky Mushroom Soup

Time: 8 hrs. 30 mins   Servings: 8
Ingredients:
2 tablespoons olive oil
1-pound fresh mushrooms, chopped
1 zucchini, cubed
1 sweet onion, chopped
1 garlic clove, chopped
1 yellow bell pepper, cored and diced
3 cups water
1/2 cup tomato sauce
Salt and pepper
2 large potatoes, peeled and cubed
2 tomatoes, peeled and diced
2 cups vegetable stock
1 lemon, juiced
1 tablespoon chopped dill

Directions:
1. Heat the oil in a pan and add the onion, garlic, and bell pepper. Cook for 5 minutes until softened, then place in a slow cooker.
2. Add the mushrooms, stock, water, zucchini, potatoes, tomatoes, and tomato sauce then sprinkle with salt and pepper.
3. Cook on low for 8 hours.
4. Add the lemon juice and chopped dill and serve warm.

Chunky Pumpkin and Kale Soup

Time: 6 hrs. 30 mins   Servings: 6
Ingredients:
1/2 teaspoon cumin seeds
Salt and pepper
1/2 red chili, chopped
2 tablespoons olive oil
2 cups pumpkin cubes
2 cups vegetable stock
1 sweet onion, chopped
1 red bell pepper, cored and diced
2 cups water
1 bunch kale, shredded

Directions:
1. Put the chili, onion, bell pepper, and olive oil in a slow cooker.
2. Add the remaining ingredients and salt and pepper.
3. Mix gently, then cook for 6 hours on low.
4. Serve warm.

White Chicken Chili Soup

Time: 7 hrs. 30 mins   **Servings: 8**

Ingredients:
1/2 teaspoon chili powder
Salt and pepper
1 yellow bell pepper, cored and diced
2 carrots, diced
1 celery stalk, diced
1 pound ground chicken
2 tablespoons olive oil
2 cups chicken stock
3 cups water
1 parsnip, diced
2 cans (15 oz.) white beans, drained

Directions:
1. Heat the oil in a pan and add the chicken. Cook for 5 minutes, stirring often, then place the meat in a slow cooker.
2. Add the remaining ingredients and sprinkle with salt and pepper.
3. Cover and cook for 7 hours on low.
4. Serve the soup either hot or cold.

Garam Masala Chicken Soup

Time: 8 hrs. 15 mins   **Servings: 8**

Ingredients:
1/2 lemongrass stalk, crushed
1/2 teaspoon cumin seeds
Salt and pepper
1 sweet onion, chopped
1 cup tomato sauce
1 bay leaf
2 garlic cloves, chopped
8 chicken drumsticks
2 tablespoons canola oil
1 teaspoon garam masala
1-pound potatoes, peeled and cubed
1 cup coconut milk
2 cups chicken stock
2 cups water

Directions:
1. Heat the canola oil in a pan and add the drumsticks. Cook until golden brown and crispy, then place in a slow cooker.
2. Add the remaining ingredients then sprinkle with salt and pepper.
3. Cook for 8 hours on low.
4. Serve the soup hot or cold.

Orange Salmon Soup

Time: 2 hrs. 15 mins   **Servings: 8**

Ingredients:
1 lemon, juiced
1 orange, juiced
1/2 teaspoon grated orange zest
Salt and pepper
1 small fennel bulb, sliced
1 cup diced tomatoes
3 salmon fillets, cubed
2 cups vegetable stock
1 sweet onion, chopped
1 garlic clove, chopped
1 celery stalk, sliced
3 cups water

Directions:
1. Mix the celery, fennel bulb, onion, garlic, tomatoes, salmon, stock and water in your slow cooker.
2. Add the remaining ingredients and sprinkle with salt and pepper.
3. Cook for 2 hours on high.
4. Serve the soup hot or cold.

Creamy Tortellini Soup

Time: 6 hrs. 15 mins   **Servings: 6**

Ingredients:
1 shallot, chopped
1 garlic clove, chopped
1/2 pound mushrooms, sliced
1 can condensed cream of mushroom soup
2 cups chicken stock
1 cup water
1/2 teaspoon dried oregano
1/2 teaspoon dried basil
1 cup evaporated milk
7 oz. cheese tortellini
Salt and pepper to taste

Directions:
1. Stir together the mushrooms, cream of mushroom soup, shallot, garlic, stock, water, dried herbs, and milk in your slow cooker.
2. Add the cheese tortellini and sprinkle with salt and pepper.
3. Cook for 6 hours on low.
4. Serve warm.

Spicy Chili Soup with Tomatillos

Time: 8 hrs. 30 mins   **Servings: 8**
Ingredients:
1 jalapeño pepper, chopped
1 can (15 oz.) black beans, drained
1 can fire roasted tomatoes
1/2 pound beef roast, cubed
10 oz. canned tomatillos, rinsed, drained and chopped
1 dried ancho chili, seeded and chopped
1 cup beef stock
4 cups water
Chopped cilantro and sour cream for serving
Salt and pepper
1 bay leaf
1 thyme sprig

Directions:
1. Mix the ancho chili, jalapeño pepper, beef roast, tomatillos, and black beans in your slow cooker.
2. Add the water, salt, tomatoes, beef stock, and pepper, and also bay leaf and thyme sprig.
3. Cook for 8 hours on low.
4. Top with chopped cilantro and a dollop of sour cream and serve warm.

Portobello Mushroom Soup

Time: 6 hrs. 15 mins   **Servings: 6**
Ingredients:
4 Portobello mushrooms, sliced
1 shallot, chopped
2 garlic cloves, chopped
1 cup diced tomatoes
1 tablespoon tomato paste
2 cups chicken stock
1 can condensed cream of mushroom soup
Salt and pepper
1/2 teaspoon cumin seeds
1 tablespoon chopped parsley
1 tablespoon chopped cilantro

Directions:
1. Mix the garlic, tomatoes, mushrooms, shallot, tomato paste, stock, and mushroom soup in a slow cooker.
2. Add the cumin seeds then sprinkle with salt and pepper.
3. Cook for 6 hours on low.
4. When done, add the chopped parsley and cilantro.
5. Serve warm.

Bouillabaisse Soup

Time: 1 hr. 30 mins   **Servings: 8**
Ingredients:
1 pound haddock fillets, cubed
1 tablespoon chopped parsley
2 cups vegetable stock
1 cup diced tomatoes
2 garlic cloves, chopped
1 red bell pepper, cored and diced
2 large potatoes, peeled and cubed
1 celery stalk, sliced
1 carrot, diced
1 fennel bulb, sliced
Salt and pepper
1 shallot, chopped
1/2 lemon, juiced

Directions:
1. Mix the bell pepper, carrot, shallot, garlic, fennel, tomatoes and stock in your slow cooker.
2. Add the lemon juice, salt, potatoes, celery, and pepper and cook on high for 1 hour.
3. Add the haddock fillets and continue cooking for 5 minutes on low.
4. Serve warm and top with chopped parsley.

Pork and Corn Soup

Time: 8 hrs. 15 mins   **Servings: 8**
Ingredients:
2 carrots, sliced
2 cups chicken stock
4 cups water
Salt and pepper
2 tablespoons chopped cilantro
1 celery stalk, sliced
2 yellow bell peppers, cored and diced
2 cups frozen sweet corn
1 pound pork roast, cubed
1 sweet onion, chopped
2 bacon slices, chopped
1 garlic clove, chopped
1/2 teaspoon cumin seeds
1/2 red chili, sliced

Directions:
1. Put the bacon, pork roast, sweet onion, and garlic in a pan and cook for 5 minutes, stirring continuously.
2. Place in the slow cooker and add the bell peppers, stock, water, sweet corn, cumin seeds, carrots, celery, red chili, salt and pepper.
3. Cook for 8 hours on low.
4. When done, add the chopped cilantro.
5. Serve warm.

CHAPTER 4

DESSERT RECIPES

Lavender Blackberry Crumble

Time: 2 hrs. 15 mins   **Servings: 6**

Ingredients:
1 teaspoon dried lavender buds
1 cup all-purpose flour
1 pinch salt
1 1/2 pounds fresh blackberries
2 tablespoons cornstarch
1 teaspoon vanilla extract
1/4 cup white sugar
1/2 cup butter, chilled and cubed

Directions:
1. Combine the vanilla, sugar, blackberries, cornstarch, and lavender in a slow cooker.
2. Mix the salt, flour, and butter in a bowl and knead lightly with your fingertips until the mixture looks combined but still crumbly.
3. Spread the mixture over the fruit and cook for 2 hours on high.
4. Allow to come to room temperature before serving.

Raspberry Brownie Cake

Time: 3 hrs. 15 mins   **Servings: 10**

Ingredients:
1 cup sugar
4 eggs
1 pinch salt
1/2 cup cocoa powder
1 1/2 cups fresh raspberries
1/2 cup all-purpose flour
1 cup butter, cubed
1 1/2 cups dark chocolate, chopped

Directions:
1. Mix the butter with chocolate in a double boiler.
2. Stir until smooth and melted.
3. Remove from heat and add the sugar and eggs.
4. Add the flour, cocoa powder, and salt, and pour the batter into your greased crock pot.
5. Top with raspberries and cover.
6. Cook for 3 hours on high.
7. Allow to cool before serving.

Apple Butter

Time: 8 hrs. 15 mins   **Servings: 12**

Ingredients:
1 cup sugar
4 eggs
1 pinch salt
4 pounds Granny Smith apples, peeled and cored
2 pounds tart apples, peeled and cored
2 cups white sugar
1 cup fresh apple juice
1 teaspoon cinnamon powder
1/2 teaspoon ground ginger

Directions:
1. Place all the ingredients in a slow cooker and mix well
2. Cover and cook on low for 8 hours.
3. When done, purée with a blender and pour into jars.
4. Seal the jars and store for up to a few months.

Pineapple Upside Down Cake

Time: 5 hrs. 15 mins   **Servings: 10**

Ingredients:
1 cup butter, softened
1/2 cup light brown sugar
1/2 teaspoon cinnamon powder
2 tablespoons butter for greasing
1 can pineapple chunks, drained
1/2 cup white sugar
2 eggs
1 cup all-purpose flour
1/2 cup ground almonds
1 teaspoon baking powder
1/4 teaspoon salt

Directions:
1. Grease the pot with butter then add the pineapple chunks.
2. For the cake, mix the softened butter, brown sugar and white sugar in a bowl. Add the eggs and stir.
3. Add the flour, almonds, baking powder and salt, as well as cinnamon.
4. Pour the mixture over the pineapple and bake for 5 hours on low.

Pure Berry Crumble

Time: 5 hrs. 15 mins   **Servings: 8**
Ingredients:
1 teaspoon lemon zest
1 cup all-purpose flour
1 pound fresh mixed berries
1 tablespoon cornstarch
1/4 cup white sugar
1/2 teaspoon baking powder
1/2 cup butter, chilled and cubed
1/4 cup cornstarch
1 pinch salt
2 tablespoons sugar
Directions:
1. In the crock pot, combine the berries, cornstarch, 1/4 cup sugar, and lemon zest.
2. In a bowl, add the flour, cornstarch, salt, and baking powder for the topping. When the mixture becomes grainy, add the butter and stir thoroughly.
3. Cover the berries with the flour mixture and cook on low for 5 hours.
4. Cool before serving.

Apple Sour Cream Crostata

Time: 6 hrs. 30 mins   **Servings: 8**
Ingredients:
1/4 cup light brown sugar
1 1/2 cups all-purpose flour
1/2 cup butter, chilled and cubed
2 pounds Granny Smith apples, peeled, cored and sliced
1 tablespoon cornstarch
1 teaspoon cinnamon powder
1 pinch salt
2 tablespoons white sugar
1/2 cup sour cream
Directions:
1. In a bowl, combine the butter, flour, white sugar, and salt. Knead well with your hands until it becomes gritty, then add the sour cream and knead again.
2. To make the dough fit your crock pot, roll it out on a surface dusted with flour.
3. Place the dough in the slow cooker.
4. To make the topping, combine the apples with cornstarch, cinnamon, and light brown sugar. Put the mixture on top of the dough.
5. Put the lid on the pot and cook on low for six hours.
6. Serve cool.

Cranberry Stuffed Apples

Time: 4 hrs. 15 mins   **Servings: 4**
Ingredients:
1/4 cup ground almonds
1/4 cup pecans, chopped
4 large Granny Smith apples
1/2 cup dried cranberries
2 tablespoons honey
1/4 teaspoon cinnamon powder
1/2 cup apple cider

Directions:
1. Core the apples, then place in the slow cooker.
2. In a bowl, combine the cranberries, honey, almonds, pecans, and cinnamon. Add cider.
3. Stuff the apples with cider mixture.
4. Cook covered for 4 hours on low.
5. Serve warm.

Autumnal Bread Pudding

Time: 5 hrs. 30 mins   **Servings: 8**
Ingredients:
16 oz. bread cubes
2 red apples, peeled and diced
2 pears, peeled and diced
1/2 cup golden raisins
1/4 cup butter, melted
2 cups whole milk
4 eggs, beaten
1/2 cup white sugar
1 teaspoon vanilla extract
1/2 teaspoon cinnamon powder

Directions:
1. In your slow cooker, combine the bread cubes, apples, pears, and raisins.
2. In a bowl, mix the butter, milk, eggs, sugar, vanilla, and cinnamon. Pour this mixture over the bread.
3. Cook covered for 5 hours on low.
4. Serve warm.

Creamy Coconut Tapioca Pudding

Time: 4 hrs. 15 mins　　　**Servings: 6**
Ingredients:
1 cup water
1 teaspoon vanilla extract
1 cup tapioca pearls
1 cup coconut flakes
2 cups coconut milk
1/2 cup coconut sugar

Directions:
1. Mix all the ingredients in your slow cooker.
2. Cover and cook for 4 hours on low.
3. Serve the pudding warm or chilled.

Rich Chocolate Peanut Butter Cake

Time: 2 hrs. 45 mins　　　**Servings: 8**
Ingredients:
1/2 teaspoon baking soda 3 eggs
3/4 cup sour cream
1/4 teaspoon salt
1 cup smooth peanut butter
1 1/2 cups all-purpose flour
1/4 cup cocoa powder
1 teaspoon baking powder
1/4 cup butter, softened
3/4 cup white sugar

Directions:
1. Mix the peanut butter, butter and sugar in a bowl until creamy.
2. Add the eggs, then add the flour, cocoa powder, baking powder, baking soda and salt.
3. Finally, add the sour cream and mix on high speed for 30 seconds.
4. Place the batter in your slow cooker and cook for 2 1/4 hours on high.
5. Serve the cake cool.

One Bowl Chocolate Cake

Time: 4 hrs. 15 mins　　　**Servings: 10**
Ingredients:
2 eggs
1 cup whole milk
1/2 cup canola oil
1 teaspoon baking powder
1 teaspoon vanilla extract
1/2 cup brewed coffee
1 teaspoon baking soda
1/2 teaspoon salt
1 1/2 cups sugar
1 1/2 cups all-purpose flour
1/2 cup cocoa powder

Directions:
1. Put all the ingredients in a bowl and give it a quick mix.
2. Pour the mixture in the crock pot and cover.
3. Cook for 4 hours on low.
4. Allow it to cool in the pot before slicing and serving.

Oat–Topped Apples

Time: 4 hrs. 15 mins　　　**Servings: 6**
Ingredients:
2 tablespoons brown sugar
1 cup rolled oats
6 Granny Smith apples
1 cup golden raisins
1/2 cup apple cider
1/4 cup all-purpose flour
1/4 cup butter, chilled and cubed

Directions:
1. Core the apples and put them in your slow cooker.
2. Combine the raisins with brown sugar and stuff the apples with this mixture.
3. For the topping, mix the oats, flour and butter until grainy.
4. Pour the topping over each apple then pour the cider in the pot.
5. Cook for 4 hours on low.
6. Serve the apples cool.

Apple Cinnamon Brioche Pudding

Time: 6 hrs. 30 mins   **Servings: 8**
Ingredients:
1 cup whole milk
4 eggs
1 teaspoon vanilla extract
1/2 teaspoon ground ginger
2 tablespoons white sugar
1 cup evaporated milk
16 oz. brioche bread, cubed
4 Granny Smith apples, peeled and cubed
1 teaspoon cinnamon powder
1 cup sweetened condensed milk

Directions:
1. Mix the brioche bread, apples, cinnamon, ginger, and sugar in your crock pot.
2. Combine the three types of milk in a bowl. Add the eggs and vanilla and mix well.
3. Pour this mix over the bread then cover the pot and cook for 6 hours on low.
4. The pudding is best served slightly warm.

Apple Cherry Cobbler

Time: 4 hrs. 30 mins   **Servings: 10**
Ingredients:
1 pound cherries, pitted
4 red apples, peeled and sliced
4 tablespoons maple syrup
2 tablespoons cornstarch
1 tablespoon lemon juice
1 1/4 cups all-purpose flour
1/2 cup butter, chilled and cubed
2 tablespoons white sugar
1/2 cup buttermilk, chilled

Directions:
1. Mix the cherries, apples, maple syrup, cornstarch and lemon juice in your crock pot.
2. For the topping, combine the flour, butter and sugar in a bowl and mix well with your fingertips until grainy.
3. Add the buttermilk and mix.
4. Pour the mixture over the fruit mixture and bake for 4 hours on low.
5. Serve the cobbler cool.

Nutty Pear Streusel

Time: 4 hrs. 15 mins   **Servings: 4**
Ingredients:
2 tablespoons melted butter
2 tablespoons brown sugar
1 pinch salt
1 teaspoon cinnamon
1/2 cup pecans, chopped
1 cup ground almonds
4 large apples, peeled and cubed
1/2 cup golden raisins
2 tablespoons all-purpose flour

Directions:
1. Combine the apples, raisins, and cinnamon in your slow cooker.
2. For the topping, mix the pecans, almonds, flour, melted butter, sugar and salt.
3. Pour this mixture over the pears and cook on low for 4 hours.
4. Serve this dessert warm.

Pumpkin Croissant Pudding

Time: 5 hrs. 15 mins   **Servings: 6**
Ingredients:
1 1/2 cups pumpkin puree
3 eggs
6 large croissants, cubed
1 teaspoon cinnamon powder
1/4 cup white sugar
1 cup skim milk

Directions:
1. Put the croissants in your crock pot.
2. Combine the milk, pumpkin puree, eggs, cinnamon and sugar in a bowl. Spread this mixture over the croissants.
3. Cover the pot and cook for 5 hours on low.
4. Serve the pudding cool.

Strawberry Fudgy Brownies

Time: 2 hrs. 15 mins   **Servings: 8**

Ingredients:

2 eggs
1/2 cup white sugar
1/4 cup cocoa powder
1 pinch salt
1 1/2 cups fresh strawberries, halved
1/2 cup all-purpose flour
1/2 cup butter, cubed
1 cup dark chocolate chips
1/2 cup applesauce

Directions:

1. Put the butter and chocolate in a double boiler and heat until melted and combined.
2. Remove from heat and add the eggs, sugar and applesauce and stir.
3. Add the cocoa powder, flour and salt, then pour the mixture into your slow cooker.
4. Top with strawberries and cook for 2 hours on high.
5. Allow to cool before cutting into cubes and serving.

Caramel Pear Pudding Cake

Time: 4 hrs. 15 mins   **Servings: 6**

Ingredients:

1/2 cup sugar
1/4 teaspoon salt
1/2 teaspoon cinnamon powder
4 ripe pears, cored and sliced
3/4 cup caramel sauce
2/3 cup all-purpose flour
1 teaspoon baking powder
1/4 cup butter, melted
1/4 cup whole milk

Directions:

1. Add the sugar, flour, baking powder, salt, and cinnamon in a bowl. Add the butter and milk and give it a fast mix.
2. Put the pears in your crock pot and top with the mixture.
3. Drizzle the mixture with caramel sauce and cook for 4 hours on low.
4. Allow the cake to cool before serving.

Walnut Apple Crisp

Time: 4 hrs. 30 mins   **Servings: 6**

Ingredients:

4 tablespoons light brown sugar
1 pinch salt
1/4 cup butter, melted
Caramel sauce for serving
1 tablespoon lemon juice
1/2 cup all-purpose flour
1 cup ground walnuts
2 tablespoons white sugar
1 tablespoon cornstarch
1 1/2 pounds Granny Smith apples, peeled, cored and sliced
1 teaspoon cinnamon powder
1 teaspoon ground ginger

Directions:

1. Combine the ginger, light brown sugar, apples, cinnamon, lemon juice and cornstarch in a slow cooker.
2. For the topping, combine the flour, walnuts, white sugar, salt and butter in a bowl.
3. Spread this mixture over the apples and cover.
4. Cook for 4 hours on low.
5. Serve the crisp cool.

Lemon Berry Cake

Time: 4 hrs. 30 mins   **Servings: 10**

Ingredients:

2 teaspoons lemon zest
4 eggs
1 cup butter, softened
1 teaspoon baking powder
1/4 teaspoon salt
1 cup fresh mixed berries
1 cup white sugar
1 teaspoon vanilla extract
1 cup all-purpose flour

Directions:

1. Combine the butter, sugar and vanilla in a bowl until creamy.
2. Add the eggs and lemon zest and mix for 1 minute on high speed.
3. Combine the baking powder, flour, and salt in a bowl, then add to your slow cooker.
4. Cover and cook for 4 hours on low.
5. Allow to cool before serving.

Silky Chocolate Fondue

Time: 2 hrs. 15 mins   **Servings: 6**
Ingredients:
2 tablespoons dark rum
1/4 cup whole milk
1 1/2 cups dark chocolate chips
1 cup heavy cream
1/4 cup sweetened condensed milk
Cut fresh fruit of your choice for serving
(strawberries, grapes, bananas, kiwi, apples, etc.)

Directions:
1. Mix the cream, two types of milk, chocolate chips, and rum in your slow cooker.
2. Cover and cook the mixture for 2 hours on low.
3. Serve the fondue with the fresh fruit for dipping.

Orange Ginger Cheesecake

Time: 7 hrs. 30 mins   **Servings: 8**
Ingredients:
Crust:
1 tablespoon grated orange zest
6 oz. graham crackers, crushed
1/2 cup butter, melted
Filling:
1 pinch salt
1 tablespoon cornstarch
1 teaspoon grated ginger
20 oz. cream cheese
1 cup sour cream
4 eggs
1 teaspoon grated orange zest
1/2 cup white sugar

Directions:
1. For the crust, combine the two ingredients together in a bowl then transfer to your crock pot and firmly press in the bottom of the pot.
2. For the filling, mix all the ingredients in a bowl, then pour the mix over the crust.
3. Cover and cook for 7 hours on low.
4. Allow the cheesecake to cool before slicing and serving.

White Chocolate Apricot Bread Pudding

Time: 5 hrs. 30 mins   **Servings: 8**
Ingredients:
1 cup white chocolate chips
2 cups milk
8 cups one day old bread cubes
1 cup dried apricots, diced
1 teaspoon vanilla extract
1 teaspoon orange zest
1 cup heavy cream
4 eggs
1/2 cup white sugar

Directions:
1. Combine the bread, apricots and chocolate chips in your slow cooker.
2. Put the milk, cream, eggs, vanilla, orange zest and sugar in a bowl and mix.
3. Pour this mixture over the bread pudding then cover the pot and cook for 5 hours on low.
4. The pudding is best served slightly warm.

Coconut Poached Pears

Time: 6 hrs. 15 mins   **Servings: 6**
Ingredients:
6 ripe but firm pears
2 cups coconut milk
2 cups water
1 cinnamon stick
1 star anise
3/4 cup coconut sugar
2 lemon rings

Directions:
1. Peel the pears, then place in your slow cooker.
2. Add the remaining ingredients and cover. Cook for 6 hours on low.
3. Allow the pears to cool in the pot before serving.

Chocolate Walnut Bread

Time: 2 hrs. 30 mins   **Servings: 8**

Ingredients:

1/2 cup canola oil
1 teaspoon vanilla extract
1 cup whole milk
3 eggs
1/4 cup sour cream
1/2 cup light brown sugar
1/4 teaspoon salt
1 teaspoon baking powder
1 cup all-purpose flour
1/2 cup cocoa powder
1 cup walnuts, chopped

Directions:

1. Mix the milk, eggs, canola oil, vanilla, sugar, and sour cream in a bowl.
2. Add the remaining ingredients and whisk, just until combined.
3. Pour the mixture in your crock pot and cook on high for 2 hours.
4. Allow it to cool in the pot before serving.

Egyptian Rice Pudding

Time: 4 hrs. 15 mins   **Servings: 6**

Ingredients:

1 vanilla pod, cut in half lengthwise
1/4 cup cold water
1/2 cup sugar
2 tablespoons cornstarch
1 1/2 cups white rice
4 cups whole milk
1 teaspoon cinnamon powder

Directions:

1. Combine the rice, milk, vanilla pod and sugar in your crock pot.
2. Cook for 3 hours on low.
3. Mix the water and cornstarch in a bowl, then pour this mixture over the rice pudding.
4. Cover and cook for 1 additional hour on low.
5. Serve the pudding warm or cook and sprinkle with cinnamon powder.

Ginger Fruit Compote

Time: 6 hrs. 30 mins   **Servings: 6**

Ingredients:

2 whole cloves
1/2 cup dried apricots, halved
2 ripe pears, peeled and cubed
2 red apples, peeled, cored and sliced
4 slices fresh pineapple, cubed
2 cups water
1 star anise
1 cup fresh orange juice
3 tablespoons light brown sugar
1 cinnamon stick

Directions:

1. Place all the ingredients in your slow cooker.
2. Cover and cook for 6 hours on low.
3. Allow to cool before serving.

Molten Chocolate Cake

Time: 2 hrs. 30 mins   **Servings: 6**

Ingredients:

1/4 cup cocoa powder
1 teaspoon baking powder
1 teaspoon vanilla extract
1 cup sugar
4 eggs
1/2 cup butter, melted
1 cup all-purpose flour
1/4 teaspoon salt

Directions:

1. Combine the eggs, butter, vanilla and sugar in a bowl until creamy.
2. Add the cocoa powder, flour, and salt and mix, but don't over-mix.
3. Pour the batter into your crock pot and cook for 2 hours on high.
4. Serve the cake warm.

Maraschino Cherry Cola Cake

Time: 4 hrs. 15 mins   **Servings: 8**
Ingredients:
1/2 cup butter, melted
1 teaspoon vanilla extract
1 cup cola
1/2 teaspoon baking powder
1/2 teaspoon baking soda
1/4 cup light brown sugar
1/4 cup cocoa powder
1/2 cup whole milk
1 1/2 cups all-purpose flour
1/4 teaspoon salt
2 cups Maraschino cherries, pitted

Directions:
1. Combine the cola, sugar, butter, vanilla and milk in a bowl.
2. Add the cocoa powder, flour, salt, baking powder and baking soda and give it a fast mix.
3. Add the cherries. Pour the mixture into the empty slow cooker and cook on low for 4 hours.
4. Allow the cake to cool before slicing and serving.

Crock Pot Crème Brulee

Time: 6 hrs. 15 mins   **Servings: 4**
Ingredients:
2 egg yolks
2 whole eggs
2 1/2 cups milk
1 1/2 cups heavy cream
2 tablespoons sugar
1 teaspoon vanilla extract
2 tablespoons maple syrup
1 cup sugar for topping
Directions:
1. Combine the egg yolks, eggs, milk, cream, vanilla, maple syrup and 2 tbsp. sugar in a bowl.
2. Pour the mixture into 4 ramekins and place the ramekins in your slow cooker.
3. Add enough water to the slow cooker to cover ¾ of the ramekins.
4. Cover the pot and cook for 6 hours on low.
5. When done, pour the remaining sugar over the crème brûlée and caramelize it using a blow torch.

No-Crust Lemon Cheesecake

Time: 6 hrs. 15 mins   **Servings: 8**
Ingredients:
4 eggs
2 tablespoons cornstarch
24 oz. cream cheese
2/3 cup white sugar
1 teaspoon vanilla extract
1/2 cup heavy cream
1 lemon, zested and juiced

Directions:
1. Put all the ingredients in a bowl and mix well.
2. Pour the batter into your greased slow cooker and cook on low for 6 hours.
3. Serve cold.

Fudgy Peanut Butter Cake

Time: 2 hrs. 15 mins   **Servings: 8**
Ingredients:
3/4 cup white sugar
1 teaspoon vanilla extract
1/2 cup smooth peanut butter
1/4 cup canola oil
1/4 cup cocoa powder
1 teaspoon baking powder
2 eggs
1/4 cup whole milk
1 cup all-purpose flour
1/4 teaspoon salt

Directions:
1. Combine the peanut butter, canola oil, sugar, vanilla and eggs in a bowl and stir until smooth and creamy.
2. Add the milk as well as the flour, cocoa powder, baking powder, and salt.
3. Pour the batter into your slow cooker and cook on high for 2 hours.
4. Allow it to cool in the pot before slicing and serving.

Spiced Rice Pudding

Time: 4 hrs. 15 mins   Servings: 6
Ingredients:
3 cups whole milk
1 star anise
1/2-inch piece of ginger, sliced
1/2 teaspoon rose water
2 whole cloves
1 cinnamon stick
1 cup Arborio rice
1/2 cup white sugar

Directions:
1. Put all the ingredients in your slow cooker.
2. Cover and cook for 4 hours on low.
3. Serve either hot or cold.

Spiced Poached Pears

Time: 6 hrs. 30 mins   Servings: 6
Ingredients;
3/4 cup white sugar
1 star anise
6 ripe but firm pears
2 cups white wine
2 cinnamon stick
1 1/2 cups water
1-inch piece of ginger, sliced
4 whole cloves
2 cardamom pods, crushed

Directions:
1. Peel and place the pears in your slow cooker.
2. Add the remaining ingredients and cook for 6 hours on low.
3. Serve the pears cool.

Tiramisu Bread Pudding

Time: 4 hrs. 15 mins   Servings: 6
Ingredients:
2 eggs
2 tablespoons cocoa powder
2 tablespoons Kahlua
1/2 cup mascarpone cheese
6 cups bread cubes
1/4 cup white sugar
2 teaspoons coffee powder
1 1/2 cups milk

Directions:
1. Mix the sugar, coffee, Kahlua, mascarpone cheese, milk and eggs in a bowl.
2. Place the bread cubes in a slow cooker, then pour the milk mixture over the bread.
3. Sprinkle with cocoa powder and cook on low for 4 hours.
4. Serve the pudding slightly warm.

Amaretti Cheesecake

Time: 6 hrs. 30 mins   Servings: 8
Ingredients:
Crust:
1/4 cup butter, melted
6 oz. Amaretti cookies, crushed
Filling:
24 oz. cream cheese
1/2 cup sour cream
4 eggs
1/2 cup white sugar
1 tablespoon vanilla extract
1 tablespoon Amaretto liqueur

Directions:
1. Combine the crushed cookies with butter, then place the mixture in your crock pot.
2. For the filling, combine the sugar, vanilla, cream cheese, sour cream, eggs, and liqueur and give it a fast mix.
3. Pour the filling over the crust and cook for 6 hours on low.
4. Let the cheesecake cool before slicing and serving.

Brandied Brioche Pudding

Time: 6 hrs. 30 mins   **Servings: 8**

Ingredients:
2 cups whole milk
1/4 cup brandy
10 oz. brioche bread, cubed
4 eggs, beaten
1 teaspoon vanilla extract
1/2 cup light brown sugar

Directions:
1. Place the brioche in a slow cooker.
2. Mix the eggs, milk, brandy, sugar and vanilla in a bowl then pour this mixture over the brioche.
3. Cover and cook on low for 6 hours.
4. Serve the pudding slightly warm.

Vanilla Bean Caramel Custard

Time: 6 hrs. 15 mins   **Servings: 6**

Ingredients:
1 cup heavy cream
2 egg yolks
1 tablespoon vanilla bean paste
2 tablespoons white sugar
1 cup white sugar for melting
4 cups whole milk
4 eggs

Directions:
1. Caramelize 1 cup of sugar in a pan until it has an amber color. Pour the caramel in a slow cooker.
2. Combine the milk, cream, egg yolks, eggs, vanilla bean paste and sugar in a bowl. Pour this mixture over the caramel.
3. Cover and cook on low for 6 hours.
4. Serve the custard cool.

Pineapple Coconut Tapioca Pudding

Time: 6 hrs. 15 mins   **Servings: 8**

Ingredients:
1 cup sweetened condensed milk
1 teaspoon vanilla extract
1 can crushed pineapple
1 1/2 cups tapioca pearls
2 cups coconut milk
1/2 cup coconut flakes

Directions:
1. Put all the ingredients in your crock pot.
2. Cover and cook on low for 6 hours.
3. Serve the pudding warm.

Cardamom Coconut Rice Pudding

Time: 6 hrs. 15 mins   **Servings: 6**

Ingredients:
1 cup coconut water
Sliced peaches for serving
1/2 cup coconut sugar
1 1/4 cups Arborio rice
2 cups coconut milk
4 cardamom pods, crushed

Directions:
1. Put all the ingredients in your crock pot.
2. Cover and cook on low for 6 hours.
3. Serve the pudding hot or cold. For more flavor, top with sliced peaches just before serving.

Rocky Road Chocolate Cake

Time: 4 hrs. 30 mins   **Servings: 10**
Ingredients:
1 1/2 cups all-purpose flour
1/2 cup cocoa powder
1 teaspoon baking soda
1/2 teaspoon salt
1/2 cup canola oil
1 cup buttermilk
1/2 cup whole milk
1 teaspoon vanilla extract
2 eggs
1/2 cup mini marshmallows
1/2 cup pecans, chopped
1/2 cup white chocolate chips

Directions:
1. Combine the cocoa powder, flour, baking soda, salt, canola oil, buttermilk, milk, vanilla and eggs in a bowl. Place the mixture in your slow cooker.
2. Top the mixture with mini marshmallows, pecans and chocolate chips.
3. Cover and cook on low for 4 hours.
4. Allow the cake to cool completely before serving.

Ricotta Lemon Cake

Time: 5 hrs. 15 mins   **Servings: 8**
Ingredients:
1 1/2 cups ricotta cheese
1/4 cup butter, melted
1/2 cup white sugar
1 teaspoon vanilla extract
1 tablespoon lemon zest
4 eggs, separated
1 1/2 cups all-purpose flour
1 1/2 teaspoons baking powder
1/4 teaspoon salt

Directions:
1. Grease your slow cooker with butter.
2. Combine the sugar, egg yolks, ricotta, butter, vanilla, and lemon zest in a bowl. Add the flour, baking powder, and salt.
3. Whip the egg whites, then add to the bowl.
4. Pour the batter in a crock pot and cook for 5 hours on low.
5. Allow the cake to cool before slicing and serving.

Sour Cream Cheesecake

Time: 4 hrs. 15 mins   **Servings: 8**
Ingredients:
Crust:
1/2 cup butter, melted
1 1/2 cups crushed graham crackers
Filling:
4 eggs
1/2 cup white sugar
12 oz. sour cream
1 tablespoon cornstarch
12 oz. cream cheese
1 tablespoon vanilla extract
1/2 teaspoon almond extract

Directions:
1. For the crust, combine the graham crackers with melted butter in a bowl, then place this mixture in a slow cooker.
2. For the filling, combine the cream cheese, cornstarch, vanilla, sour cream, eggs, sugar, and almond extract in a bowl. Pour the mixture over the crust.
3. Cook on low for 4 hours.
4. Allow to cool before slicing and serving.

Maple Roasted Pears

Time: 6 hrs. 15 mins   **Servings: 4**
Ingredients:
1 teaspoon grated ginger
1 cinnamon stick
1/4 cup white wine
1/2 cup water
1/4 cup maple syrup
2 cardamom pods, crushed
4 ripe pears, peeled and cored

Directions:
1. Put all the ingredients in your slow cooker.
2. Cover and cook on low for 6 hours.
3. Allow to cool before serving.

Apple Granola Crumble

Time: 6 hrs. 15 mins   **Servings: 4**

Ingredients:
2 tablespoons honey
1 1/2 cups granola
4 red apples, peeled, cored and sliced
1/2 teaspoon cinnamon powder

Directions:
1. Mix the apples and honey in your crock pot.
2. Top with the granola and sprinkle with cinnamon.
3. Cover and cook on low for 6 hours.
4. Serve the crumble warm.

Mixed-Nut Brownies

Time: 4 hrs. 15 mins   **Servings: 12**

Ingredients:
1 cup white sugar
3 eggs
8 oz. dark chocolate, chopped
1/2 cup butter
1/2 cup cocoa powder
1/2 teaspoon salt
1 teaspoon vanilla extract
1 cup all-purpose flour
1 cup mixed nuts, chopped

Directions:
1. Melt the chocolate and butter in a double boiler, stirring to combine.
2. Remove from heat and add the flour, cocoa powder, eggs, vanilla, and salt and stir gently.
3. Add the nuts, then pour the batter into your slow cooker.
4. Cover and cook for 4 hours on low.
5. Allow to cool before cutting into squares.

Peanut Butter Chocolate Chip Bars

Time: 2 hrs. 15 mins   **Servings: 12**

Ingredients:
2 eggs
1 cup light brown sugar
1 cup dark chocolate chips
1 cup pecans, chopped
1 cup all-purpose flour
1/2 cup butter, melted
1/2 cup smooth peanut butter
1/4 teaspoon salt

Directions:
1. Mix the butter, peanut butter, eggs and brown sugar in a bowl until creamy and smooth.
2. Add the flour and salt, then place the mixture in a slow cooker.
3. Add chocolate chips and pecans and cook on high for 2 hours.
4. Allow to cool before slicing and serving.

Golden Raisin Brioche Pudding

Time: 2 hrs. 30 mins   **Servings: 6**

Ingredients:
2 tablespoons brandy
1/4 cup white sugar
4 eggs
6 cups brioche cubes
1 cup golden raisins
2 cups whole milk

Directions:
1. Combine the brioche cubes and raisins in a slow cooker.
2. Mix the milk, brandy, eggs, and sugar in a bowl, then pour over the brioche.
3. Cover and cook on high for 2 hours.
4. Serve warm.

Coconut Condensed Milk Custard

Time: 5 hrs. 15 mins   **Servings: 6**
Ingredients:
1 1/4 cups sweetened condensed milk
1 tablespoon vanilla extract
6 eggs
1 cup evaporated milk
1 can (15 oz.) coconut milk
1 teaspoon lime zest

Directions:
1. Combine the eggs, coconut milk, condensed milk, vanilla, lime zest and evaporated milk in a bowl.
2. Place the mixture in the slow cooker.
3. Cover and cook on low for 5 hours.
4. Allow to cool before serving.

Peppermint Chocolate Clusters

Time: 4 hrs. 15 mins   **Servings: 20**
Ingredients:
1/2 cup milk chocolate chips
1 teaspoon peppermint extract
2 cups pretzels, chopped
1 1/2 cups dark chocolate chips
1 cup pecans, chopped

Directions:
1. Mix all the ingredients in your slow cooker.
2. Cover and cook on low for 4 hours.
3. When done, drop small clusters of batter onto a baking tray lined with parchment paper.
4. Allow to cool then serve.

Buttery Chocolate Cake

Time: 4 hrs. 15 mins   **Servings: 10**
Ingredients:
4 eggs
1 cup dark chocolate, melted and cooled
1/2 cup sour cream
3/4 cup butter, softened
3/4 cup light brown sugar
1 1/2 teaspoons baking powder
1/4 teaspoon salt
1 1/4 cups all-purpose flour
1/4 cup cocoa powder

Directions:
1. Stir the butter and sugar in a bowl until creamy. Add the eggs, then stir in the melted chocolate and sour cream.
2. Add the flour, cocoa powder, baking powder, and salt.
3. Place the batter in your slow cooker and cook on low for 4 hours.
4. Allow the cake to cool before serving.

S'Mores Fondue

Time: 1 hr. 15 mins   **Servings: 6**
Ingredients:
1/2 teaspoon all-spice powder
1 1/2 cups dark chocolate chips
1 cup mini marshmallows
1/2 cup caramel sauce
1/2 cup heavy cream
1 can (15 oz.) sweetened condensed milk
Pretzels or fresh fruit for serving

Directions:
1. Combine the milk, caramel sauce, cream, chocolate chips, all-spice powder, and marshmallows in your slow cooker.
2. Cover and cook for 1 hour on high.
3. Serve the fondue warm with pretzels or fresh fruit.

Double Chocolate Cake

Time: 4 hrs. 15 mins   **Servings: 8**
Ingredients:
1/4 teaspoon salt
1/4 cup cocoa powder
1 1/2 cups all-purpose flour
1 1/2 teaspoons baking powder
1 cup dark chocolate chips
4 eggs
1 teaspoon vanilla extract
1/2 cup vegetable oil
1 cup water
1 cup sour cream

Directions:
1. Combine the flour, baking powder, salt, and cocoa powder in a bowl.
2. Add the water, oil, sour cream, eggs, vanilla extract and stir to combine.
3. Pour the batter into your slow cooker and top with chocolate chips.
4. Cover and cook on low for 4 hours.
5. Allow to cool before serving.

Saucy Apples and Pears

Time: 6 hrs. 15 mins   **Servings: 6**
Ingredients:
1/4 cup light brown sugar
1 cup water
1 cinnamon stick
1/4 cup butter
1 cup apple juice
1 star anise
4 ripe pears, peeled, cored and sliced
2 Granny Smith apples, peeled, cored and sliced

Directions:
1. Mix all the ingredients in the crock pot.
2. Cover and cook on low for 6 hours.
3. Allow to cool in the pot before serving.

Blueberry Dumpling Pie

Time: 5 hrs. 30 mins   **Servings: 8**
Ingredients:
1/4 cup light brown sugar
1 tablespoon lemon zest
1/2 cup butter, chilled and cubed
1 1/2 cups all-purpose flour
2 tablespoons white sugar
2/3 cup buttermilk, chilled
1 1/2 pounds fresh blueberries
2 tablespoons cornstarch
1/2 teaspoon salt
1 teaspoon baking powder
Directions:
1. Combine the cornstarch, blueberries, brown sugar and lemon zest in your slow cooker.
2. For the dumpling topping, put the flour, salt, sugar, baking powder, and butter in a bowl and mix until sandy.
3. Add the buttermilk and stir briskly.
4. Pour the batter over the blueberries and cook on low for 5 hours.
5. Allow to cool completely before serving.

Dried Fruit Rice Pudding

Time: 6 hrs. 15 mins   **Servings: 8**
Ingredients:
1/2 cup dried apricots, chopped
1/4 cup dried cranberries
1/2 cup white sugar
3 cups whole milk
2 cups white rice
1/2 cup golden raisins
1 1/4 cups heavy cream
1 cinnamon stick

Directions:
1. Combine the rice, milk, cream, raisins, apricots, cranberries, sugar, and cinnamon in your crock pot.
2. Cover and cook on low for 6 hours.
3. Serve warm.

CHAPTER 5

BEAN AND GRAIN RECIPES

Apple Bean Pot

Time: 3½ to 4½ hours   **Serves: 12**
Ingredients:
3 tart apples, peeled and chopped
½ cup ketchup or barbecue sauce
1 55-ounce can baked beans, well-drained
1 large onion, chopped
½ cup firmly packed brown sugar
Hot dogs or chopped ham chunks (optional)
1 package smoky cocktail sausages

Directions:
1. Put beans in crock pot.
2. Add onions and apples then mix well.
3. Add ketchup or barbecue sauce, brown sugar, and meat, then mix.
4. Cover and heat on low for 3 to 4 hours, and then on high 30 minutes.

Chili Boston Baked Beans

Time: 6 to 8 hours   **Serves: 20**
Ingredients:
2 tart apples, diced
1 cup chili sauce
1 cup raisins
2 small onions, diced
3 teaspoons dry mustard
½ cup sweet pickle relish
1 cup chopped ham or crumbled bacon
2 15-ounce cans baked beans

Directions:
1. Combine together all the ingredients.
2. Cover and cook on low for 6 to 8 hours. Serve

Never-Fail Rice

Time: 2 to 6 hours   **Serves: 6**
Ingredients:
2 cups water
½ tablespoon butter
½ teaspoon salt
1 cup long-grain rice, uncooked

Directions:
1. Put all the ingredients in small crock pot.
2. Cover and cook on low for 4 to 6 hours, or on high for 2 to 3 hours, or until rice is just fully cooked.
3. Serve.

Herbed Rice

Time: 4 to 6 hours   **Serves: 6**
Ingredients:
1 teaspoon dried rosemary
½ teaspoon dried marjoram
1 tablespoon butter or margarine
3 chicken bouillon cubes
3 cups water
1½ cups long-grain rice, uncooked
¼ cup onions, diced
¼ cup dried parsley, chopped
½ cup slivered almonds (optional)

Directions:
1. Combine the chicken bouillon cubes and water.
2. Mix all the ingredients in crock pot.
3. Cook on low for 4 to 6 hours, or until rice is fully cooked.

Wild Rice

Time: 2½ to 3 hours   **Serves: 5**

Ingredients:

1 tablespoon oil
½ teaspoon salt
½ cup sliced fresh mushrooms
½ cup diced onions
½ cup diced green or red bell peppers
¼ teaspoon black pepper
1 cup wild rice, uncooked
2½ cups fat-free, low-sodium chicken broth

Directions:

1. Put the rice and vegetables in crock pot. Pour oil, salt, and pepper over vegetables and mix.
2. Heat the chicken broth. Pour over all the ingredients in crock pot.
3. Cover and cook on high for 2½ to 3 hours, or until rice is soft and liquid is absorbed. Serve.

Hometown Spanish Rice

Time: 2 to 4 hours   **Serves: 6 to 8**

Ingredients:

1 large onion, chopped
1 bell pepper, chopped
2 cups long-grain rice, cooked
Grated Parmesan cheese (optional)
1 (28-ounce) can stewed tomatoes with juice
1 pound bacon, cooked and broken into bite-size pieces

Directions:

1. Heat the onion and pepper in a small nonstick frying pan until soft.
2. Spray interior of the crock pot with nonstick cooking spray.
3. Put all ingredients in the crock pot.
4. Cover and cook on low for 4 hours, or on high for 2 hours, or until heated through.
5. Add Parmesan cheese before serving (optional).

Risi Bisi (Peas and Rice)

Time: 2½ to 3½ hours   **Serves: 6**

Ingredients:

2 garlic cloves, minced
2 14.5-ounce cans reduced-sodium chicken broth
⅓ cup water
¾ teaspoon Italian seasoning
½ cup frozen baby peas, thawed
¼ cup grated Parmesan cheese
1½ cups converted long-grain white rice, uncooked
¾ cup chopped onions
½ teaspoon dried basil leaves

Directions:

1. Put the rice, onions, and garlic in crock pot.
2. In saucepan, combine the chicken broth and water then boil. Add Italian seasoning and basil leaves.
3. Stir into rice mixture.
4. Cover and cook on low for 2 to 3 hours, or until liquid is absorbed.
5. Add peas, then cover and cook for 30 minutes. Top with cheese. Serve.

Rice 'n Beans 'n Salsa

Time: 4 to 10 hours   **Serves: 6 to 8**

Ingredients:

1 (14-ounce / 397-g) chicken broth
1 quart salsa, your choice of heat
1 cup water
½ teaspoon garlic powder
1 cup long-grain white or brown rice, uncooked
2 16-ounce cans black or navy beans, drained

Directions:

1. Put all the ingredients in crock pot. Mix well.
2. Cover and cook on low for 8 to 10 hours, or on high for 4 hours.

Red Bean and Brown Rice Stew

Time: 6 hours   **Serves: 6**

Ingredients:
¾ cup brown rice, uncooked
4 cups water
2 cups dried red beans
1 large onion, cut into chunks
1 tablespoon cumin
6 carrots

Directions:
1. Put the dried beans in crock pot and cover with water. Allow to soak for 8 hours or overnight, then drain.
2. Return soaked beans to cooker. Add all the remaining ingredients.
3. Cover and cook on low for 6 hours.

Wild Rice Pilaf

Time: 3½ to 5 hours   **Serves: 6**

Ingredients:
2 cups water
1 (14-ounce / 397-g) chicken broth
1½ cups wild rice, uncooked
½ cup finely chopped onion
½ teaspoon dried thyme leaves
1 (4-ounce / 113-g) can sliced mushrooms, drained

Directions:
1. Spray crock pot with nonstick cooking spray.
2. Wash the rice and drain well then put rice, onion, chicken broth, and water in crock pot. Stir well.
3. Cover and cook on high for 3 to 4 hours.
4. Add mushrooms and thyme and mix gently.
5. Cover and cook on low for 30 to 60 minutes longer, or until wild rice is soft.

Broccoli-Rice Casserole

Time: 3 to 4 hours   **Serves: 6**

Ingredients
1 cup minute rice, uncooked
1 8-ounce jar processed cheese spread
1 1-pound package frozen chopped broccoli
1 10¾-ounce can cream of mushroom soup

Directions:
1. Combine all the ingredients in crock pot.
2. Cover and cook on high for 3 to 4 hours, or until rice and broccoli are soft but not mushy or dry.

Flavorful Fruited Rice

Time: 2 hours   **Serves: 4**

Ingredients
¼ cup chopped dried apricots
2 cups chicken broth
¼ cup dried cranberries
⅓ cup chopped onion
1 (6-ounce) package long-grain and wild rice mixture

Directions:
1. Spray a small frying pan with nonstick cooking spray.
2. Add chopped onions and cook on medium heat about 5 minutes.
3. Put onions and the remaining ingredients in the crock pot, as well as the seasonings. Stir well to dissolve seasonings.
4. Cover and cook on high for 2 hours.
5. Serve.

Cheddar Rice

Time: 2 to 3 hours   **Serves: 8 to 10**
Ingredients:
½ teaspoon pepper
1 teaspoon salt
5 cups water
2 cups shredded cheddar cheese
1 cup slivered almonds (optional)
2 cups brown rice, uncooked
3 tablespoons butter
½ cup thinly sliced green onions or shallots

Directions:
1. Put rice, butter, green onion, and salt in crock pot.
2. Boil the water and pour over rice mixture.
3. Cover and cook on high for 2 to 3 hours, or until rice is tender and liquid is absorbed.
4. Five minutes before serving, stir in pepper and cheese.
5. Garnish with slivered almonds, if you wish.

Makes-A-Meal Baked Beans

Time: 3 hours   **Serves: 6 to 8**
Ingredients:
1 pound ground beef
½ cup chopped onions
½ teaspoon taco seasoning, or more
1 or 2 15-ounce can(s) pork and beans
¾ cup barbecue sauce

Directions:
1. Heat the ground beef and onions in a nonstick pan. Drain.
2. Combine all the ingredients in the crock pot, including the browned ground beef and onions.
3. Cover and cook on low setting for 3 hours.
4. Serve.

Refried Beans with Bacon

Time: 5 hours   **Serves: 8**
Ingredients:
2 garlic cloves, minced
2 cups dried red or pinto beans
6 cups water
1 teaspoon salt
½ pound (227 g) bacon
Shredded cheese
1 large tomato or 1 pint tomato juice

Directions:
1. Put the beans, water, garlic, tomato, and salt in crock pot.
2. Cover and cook on high for 5 hours, stirring occasionally. When the beans become tender, drain off some water.
3. Cook the bacon in a pan, then drain and crumble. Add half of bacon and 3 tablespoons drippings to beans, then stir.
4. Blend the beans with a blender. Fry the bean mixture in the remaining bacon drippings. Add more salt.
5. Sprinkle the rest of the bacon and shredded cheese on top of beans.

No-Meat Baked Beans

Time: 6½ to 9½ hours   **Serves: 8 to 10**
Ingredients:

1 small onion, chopped	¾ cup ketchup
½ cup brown sugar	¾ cup water
1 teaspoon dry mustard	6 cups water
3 tablespoons dark molasses	1 teaspoon salt
1 pound dried navy beans	

Directions:
1. Soak beans in water overnight. Cook beans in water until tender, about 1½ hours. Drain, discarding bean water.
2. Add all ingredients in the crock pot. Mix well.
3. Cover and cook on low for 5 to 8 hours, or until beans are well-flavored.

Bean Serve

Time: 6 to 8 hours   **Serves: 12**

Ingredients:

1 tablespoon garlic powder

1 tablespoon parsley flakes

1 tablespoon dried oregano

2 cups diced carrots

2 (15-ounce) cans diced tomatoes

1 tablespoon ground cumin

2 (15-ounce) cans kidney beans, drained and rinsed

2 (15-ounce) cans pinto beans, drained and rinsed

2 cups water

1 cup minced onions

2 cups diced celery

1 tablespoon salt

Directions:

1. Place beans with onions in a nonstick skillet over medium heat. Add celery and carrots and cook. Place in crock pot.

2. Add the remaining ingredients. Stir to mix well.

3. Cover and cook on low for 6 to 8 hours.

4. Serve.

Pizza Rice

Time: 6 to 10 hours   **Serves: 6**

Ingredients:

2½ cups water

2 cups rice, uncooked

3 cups chunky pizza sauce

4 ounces pepperoni, sliced

1 cup shredded mozzarella cheese

1 (7-ounce) can mushrooms, undrained

Directions:

1. Mix rice, sauce, water, mushrooms, and pepperoni.

2. Cover and cook on low for 10 hours, or on high for 6 hours.

3. Sprinkle with cheese before serving.

Easy Wheat Berries

Time: 2 hours   **Serves: 4 to 6**

Ingredients:

½ cup dried raisins

1 (14½-ounce / 411-g) can vegetable broth

½ to 1 cup water

1 cup wheat berries

1 cup couscous or small pasta like orzo

Directions:

1. Cover wheat berries with water and soak for 2 hours before cooking. Place wheat berries into the crock pot.

2. Mix with the remaining ingredients in the crock pot.

3. Cover and cook on low until liquid is absorbed and berries are soft, about 2 hours.

Arroz con Queso

Time: 6 to 9 hours   **Serves: 6 to 8**

Ingredients:

1 tablespoon oil

3 garlic cloves, minced

1½ cups long-grain rice, uncooked

2 cups shredded Monterey Jack cheese, divided

1 teaspoon salt

1 large onion, finely chopped

1 cup cottage cheese

1 (4¼-ounce) can chopped green chili peppers, drained

1 (14½-ounce can whole tomatoes, mashed

1 (15-ounce) can Mexican style beans, undrained

Directions:

1. Stir together all ingredients except 1 cup of Monterey Jack cheese. Pour into a well-greased crock pot.

2. Cover and cook on low for 6 to 9 hours.

3. Sprinkle with the remaining cheese before serving.

Barbecued Lentils

Time: 6 to 8 hours   **Serves: 8**

Ingredients:

2 cups barbecue sauce

3½ cups water

1 pound (454 g) dry lentils

1 package vegetarian hot dogs, sliced

Directions:

1. Mix all the ingredients in crock pot.

2. Cover and cook on low for 6 to 8 hours.

3. Serve

Bacon and Beef Calico Beans

Time: 2 to 6 hours   **Serves: 10**

Ingredients:

¼ to ½ pound bacon

1 pound ground beef

1 medium onion, chopped

1 (32-ounce) can pork and beans

1 (16-ounce) can Northern beans, drained

1 (14½-ounce) can French-cut green beans, drained

½ cup brown sugar

½ cup ketchup

½ teaspoon salt

2 tablespoons cider vinegar

1 tablespoon prepared mustard

Directions:

1. Heat the bacon, ground beef, and onion in a pan until soft, then drain.

2. Mix all the ingredients in the crock pot.

3. Cover and cook on low for 5 to 6 hours, or on high for 2 to 3 hours.

4. Serve.

Smoky Beans

Time: 4 to 6 hours   **Serves: 10 to 12**

Ingredients:

1 tablespoon prepared mustard

2 tablespoons brown sugar

1 (16-ounce) can kidney beans, drained

1 cup ketchup

1 teaspoon salt

1 large onion, chopped

1 pound ground beef, browned

1 (15-ounce) can pork and beans

2 tablespoons hickory-flavored barbecue sauce

1 (15-ounce) can ranch-style beans, drained

½ to 1 pound small smoked sausage links (optional)

Directions:

1. Heat the ground beef and onion in a pan. Place into crock pot and set on high.

2. Add the remaining ingredients and mix well.

3. Reduce heat to low and cook for 4 to 6 hours. Before serving, use a paper towel to absorb oil that's risen to the top.

Pineapple Baked Beans

Time: 4 to 8 hours   **Serves: 6 to 8**

Ingredients:

1 pound (454 g) ground beef

1 (28-ounce) can baked beans

1 (8-ounce) can pineapple tidbits, drained

1 (4½-ounce) can sliced mushrooms, drained

1 large onion, chopped

1 large green pepper, chopped

½ cup barbecue sauce

2 tablespoons soy sauce

1 clove garlic, minced

½ teaspoon salt

¼ teaspoon pepper

Directions:

1. Heat the ground beef in a pan. Place in a crock pot.

2. Add the remaining ingredients and mix well.

3. Cover and cook on low for 4 to 8 hours. Serve.

CHAPTER 6

BEVERAGE RECIPES

Mulled Wine

Time: 2 hrs. 15 mins   **Servings: 8**
Ingredients:
1/4 cup light brown sugar
1 small orange, sliced
6 cups sweet red wine
4 whole cloves
2 star anise
1 cup apple cider
1 cinnamon stick
4 cardamom pods, crushed

Directions:
1. Put all the ingredients in your slow cooker.
2. Cover and cook for 2 hours on high.
3. Serve warm.

Rosemary Mulled Cider

Time: 3 hrs. 15 mins   **Servings: 6**
Ingredients:
1 cup fresh or frozen cranberries
1 cinnamon stick
2 whole cloves
1 rosemary sprig
4 cups apple cider
2 cups rose wine
1/2 cup sugar

Directions:
1. Place all the ingredients in your slow cooker.
2. Cover and cook for 3 hours on low.
3. Serve warm.

Cranberry Spiced Tea

Time: 2 hrs. 15 mins   **Servings: 6**

Ingredients:
1/2 cup sugar
2 cinnamon stick
4 cups water
2 cardamom pods, crushed
1 lemon, sliced
1 cup strong brewed black tea
1 cup cranberry juice
2 star anise
Directions:
1. Put all the ingredients in your slow cooker.
2. Cook on high for 2 hours.
3. Serve the tea warm.

Gingerbread Hot Chocolate

Time: 2 hrs. 15 mins   **Servings: 8**
Ingredients:
1 cup sweetened condensed milk
2 tablespoons cocoa powder
2 cinnamon stick
2 tablespoons maple syrup
6 cups whole milk
1 cup dark chocolate chips
1/2 teaspoon ground ginger
1 pinch salt

Directions:
1. Put all the ingredients in your slow cooker.
2. Cover and cook for 2 hours on high.
3. Serve warm.

Gingerbread Mocha Drink

Time: 1 hr. 45 mins   **Servings: 6**
Ingredients:
1/2 cup sweetened condensed milk
1/4 cup light brown sugar
3 cups whole milk
1/4 teaspoon cardamom powder
2 cups strongly brewed coffee
1/2 teaspoon ground ginger
1/4 teaspoon cinnamon powder

Directions:
1. Put all the ingredients in a slow cooker.
2. Cover and cook for 1 1/2 hours on low.
3. Serve warm.

Apple Chai Tea

Time: 4 hrs. 15 mins   **Servings: 8**
Ingredients:
1 star anise
2 whole cloves
1/3 cup sugar
2 red apples, cored and diced
4 cups brewed black tea
2 cardamom pods, crushed
4 cups fresh apple juice
2 cinnamon stick

Directions:
1. Put all the ingredients in your crock pot.
2. Cook the tea for 4 hours on low.
3. Serve warm.

Salted Caramel Milk Steamer

Time: 2 hrs. 15 mins   **Servings: 6**
Ingredients:
1 cup caramel sauce
1/4 teaspoon salt
4 cups whole milk
1 teaspoon vanilla extract
1 cup heavy cream
1/4 teaspoon ground ginger

Directions:
1. Put all the ingredients in your crock pot.
2. Cover and cook for 2 hours on low.
3. Pour into glasses or mugs and serve.

Ginger Pumpkin Latte

Time: 3 hrs. 15 mins   **Servings: 6**
Ingredients:
1 cinnamon stick
1 pinch nutmeg
1 cup brewed coffee
1/4 cup dark brown sugar
4 cups whole milk
1 cup pumpkin purée
1 teaspoon ground ginger

Directions:
1. Put all the ingredients in a slow cooker.
2. Cover and cook for 3 hours on low.
3. Serve warm.

Hot Caramel Apple Drink

Time: 2 hrs. 15 mins   Servings: 8
Ingredients:
1 cup light rum
6 cups apple cider
1 cup apple liqueur
2 cinnamon stick
1/2 cup caramel syrup
2 red apples, cored and diced

Directions:
1. Combine all the ingredients in your slow cooker.
2. Cover and cook for 2 hours on low.
3. Serve warm.

Apple Bourbon Punch

Time: 2 hrs. 15 mins   Servings: 4
Ingredients:
2 whole cloves
1/4 cup light brown sugar
3 cups apple cider
2 cinnamon stick
1 cup bourbon
1/2 cup fresh or frozen cranberries

Directions:
1. Mix all the ingredients in your crock pot
2. Cook for 2 hours on low.
3. Serve hot.

Spiced White Chocolate

Time: 1 hrs. 45 mins   Servings: 6
Ingredients:
1 pinch nutmeg
1 cup white chocolate chips
1 star anise
1/2-inch piece of ginger, sliced
1 cinnamon stick
4 cups whole milk
1 cup sweetened condensed milk

Directions:
1. Mix all the ingredients in your crock pot.
2. Cover and cook for 1 1/2 hours on low.
3. Serve hot.

Maple Bourbon Mulled Cider

Time: 1 hrs. 45 mins   Servings: 6
Ingredients:
2 star anise
1/2 cup fresh apple juice
1/4 cup maple syrup
5 cups apple cider
1/2 cup bourbon

Directions:
1. Combine all the ingredients in your slow cooker.
2. Cover and cook for 1 1/2 hours on low.
3. Serve hot.

Autumn Punch

Time: 4 hrs. 15 mins **Servings: 8**
Ingredients:
1 cup cranberry juice
6 cups red wine
1 cup bourbon
1 ripe pear, cored and sliced
1 cinnamon stick
2 whole cloves
1 vanilla bean, split in half lengthwise
2 red apples, cored and diced

Directions:
1. Mix all the ingredients in your slow cooker.
2. Cover and cook for 4 hours on low.
3. Serve hot or cool.

Boozy Hot Chocolate

Time: 4 hrs. 15 mins **Servings: 6**
Ingredients:
1 cup dark chocolate chips
2 tablespoons maple syrup
1 cinnamon stick
1/2 cup dark rum
4 cups whole milk
1 cup sweetened condensed milk

Directions:
1. Combine all the ingredients in your slow cooker.
2. Cover and cook for 4 hours on low.
3. Serve warm.

Hot Spicy Apple Cider

Time: 3 hrs. 15 mins **Servings: 6**
Ingredients:
1 star anise
2 cinnamon stick
5 cups apple cider
1 cup white rum
1 orange, sliced
1/4 teaspoon chili powder

Directions:
1. Mix all the ingredients in your crock pot.
2. Cover and cook for 3 hours on low.
3. Serve warm.

Vanilla Latte

Time: 2 hrs. 15 mins **Servings: 6**
Ingredients:
1/4 cup sweetened condensed milk
2 cups brewed coffee
1 vanilla pod, split in half lengthwise
4 cups whole milk

Directions:
1. Mix all the ingredients in your crock pot.
2. Cover and cook for 2 hours on low.
3. Serve warm.

Apple Ginger Delight

Time: 1 hr. 45 mins   **Servings: 6**
Ingredients:
1/2 cup bourbon
1-inch piece of ginger, sliced
1 teaspoon dark molasses
4 cups apple cider
1 cup ginger beer
1/4 cup light brown sugar

Directions:
1. Mix all the ingredients in your slow cooker.
2. Cover and cook on low for 1 1/2 hours.
3. Serve hot.

Citrus Bourbon Cocktail

Time: 3 hrs. 15 mins   **Servings: 6**
Ingredients:
1/4 cup sugar
1 cinnamon stick
1 small grapefruit, sliced
1 small orange, sliced
1 lemon, sliced
4 cups apple cider
1 cup fresh orange juice
1 cup bourbon

Directions:
1. Mix all the ingredients in your crock pot.
2. Cover and cook on low for 3 hours.
3. Serve warm.

Eggnog Latte

Time: 2 hrs. 15 mins   **Servings: 6**
Ingredients:
1 cup whole milk
1/4 cup light brown sugar
2 cups brewed coffee
3 cups eggnog
1 teaspoon vanilla extract
1 pinch nutmeg

Directions:
1. Mix all the ingredients in your slow cooker.
2. Cook on low for 2 hours.
3. Serve hot or cold.

Lemonade Cider

Time: 1 hr. 30 mins   **Servings: 6**
Ingredients:
1 large lemon, sliced
5 cups apple cider
1/4 cup honey
1 cup ginger beer

Directions:
1. Mix all the ingredients in your slow cooker.
2. Cover and cook for 1 1/4 hours on low.
3. Serve the cider hot or cold.

Spiced Pumpkin Toddy

Time: 3 hrs. 15 mins   **Servings: 6**
Ingredients:
2 cups water
1/4 cup maple syrup
1 cinnamon stick
1/2 cup pumpkin purée
1 cup bourbon
2 cups apple cider
2 cardamom pods, crushed
1 star anise
2 orange peels

Directions:
1. Mix all the ingredients in your slow cooker.
2. Cover and cook for 3 hours on low.
3. Serve warm.

Raspberry Hot Chocolate

Time: 2 hrs. 15 mins   **Servings: 8**
Ingredients:
1 pinch salt
1 cup heavy cream
6 cups whole milk
1/4 cup cocoa powder
1 cup sweetened condensed milk
1/2 cup seedless raspberry jam

Directions:
1. Mix all the ingredients in your crock pot.
2. Cover and cook for 2 hours on low.
3. Serve hot.

Nutella Hot Chocolate

Time: 4 hrs. 15 mins   **Servings: 6**
Ingredients:
1 cinnamon stick
5 cups whole milk
1/4 cup heavy cream
3/4 cup Nutella spread

Directions:
1. Combine all the ingredients in your slow cooker.
2. Cover and cook for 4 hours on low.
3. Serve the chocolate hot.

Mulled Cranberry Punch

Time: 3 hrs. 15 mins   **Servings: 8**
Ingredients:
3 cups apple cider
1/2 cup bourbon
1 star anise
1/2 cup maple syrup
4 cups cranberry juice
1 cup fresh or frozen cranberries
2 whole cloves
1 cinnamon stick

Directions:
1. Mix all the ingredients in your crock pot.
2. Cover and cook for 3 hours on low.
3. Serve hot or cold.

Citrus Green Tea

Time: 1 hr. 45 mins   **Servings: 6**
Ingredients:
1 lemon, sliced
1/4 cup honey
5 cups brewed green tea
1 cup fresh orange juice
1/2-inch piece of ginger, sliced

Directions:
1. Mix all the ingredients in your slow cooker.
2. Cover and cook on low for 1 1/2 hours.
3. Serve the green tea hot or cold.

Mulled Pink Wine

Time: 2 hrs. 15 mins   **Servings: 6**
Ingredients:
1/4 cup honey
2 cardamom pods, crushed
6 cups rosé wine
1 cup fresh raspberries

Directions:
1. Mix all the ingredients in your slow cooker.
2. Cover and cook on low for 2 hours.
3. Serve warm.

Whiskey Pumpkin Drink

Time: 2 hrs. 15 mins   **Servings: 6**
Ingredients:
3 cups water
1 cinnamon stick
1/4 cup maple syrup
1 cup ginger ale
1 cup whiskey
1/2 cup pumpkin purée

Directions:
1. Combine all the ingredients in a slow cooker
2. Cook for 2 hours on low.
3. Serve hot or cold.

Black Tea Punch

Time: 4 hrs. 15 mins   **Servings: 8**
Ingredients:
1 lemon, sliced
2 cups apple juice
1 orange, sliced
4 cups brewed black tea
1/4 cup sugar
2 cups cranberry juice
1 cinnamon stick

Directions:
1. Mix all the ingredients in your slow cooker.
2. Cover and cook for 4 hours on low.
3. Serve warm.

Cherry Cider

Time: 1 hr. 45 mins   **Servings: 8**
Ingredients:
1 star anise
2 cinnamon stick
6 cups apple cider
2 cups cherry juice

Directions:
1. Mix all the ingredients in your slow cooker.
2. Cook on low for 1 1/2 hours.
3. Serve warm.

Spiced Coffee

Time: 2 hrs. 15 mins   **Servings: 6**
Ingredients:
1/4 cup sugar
1 cinnamon stick
2 whole cloves
2 cardamom pods, crushed
1 star anise
6 cups brewed coffee
1/4 cup chocolate syrup

Directions:
1. Mix the ingredients in a slow cooker
2. Cook for 2 hours on low.
2. Serve warm.

Chocolate Hot Coffee

Time: 3 hrs. 15 mins   **Servings: 6**
Ingredients:
1/2 cup chocolate syrup
1/2 cup heavy cream
4 cups brewed coffee
1 cup dark chocolate chips

Directions:
1. Mix all the ingredients in your crock pot.
2. Cover and cook for 3 hours on low.
3. Serve hot.

Kahlua Coffee

Time: 1 hr. 15 mins   **Servings: 6**
Ingredients:
2 cups water
1/4 cup Kahlua
2 cups whole milk
2 teaspoons instant powder
1 teaspoon vanilla extract
1/4 cup sugar
2 cups heavy cream

Directions:
1. Mix all the ingredients in your slow cooker.
2. Cover and cook on low for 1 hour.
3. Serve warm.

Peachy Cider

Time: 4 hrs. 15 mins   **Servings: 6**
Ingredients:
1 star anise
2 cups apple cider
1 cinnamon stick
2 cups peach nectar
2 tablespoons light brown sugar
2 cups apple juice
1 pinch nutmeg
2 cardamom pods, crushed

Directions:
1. Mix all the ingredients in your slow cooker.
2. Cover and cook for 4 hours on low.
3. Serve warm.

Ginger Tea

Time: 1 hr. 15 mins   **Servings: 6**
Ingredients:
1 lemon, sliced
1/4 cup honey
1-inch piece of ginger, sliced
6 cups water
6 green tea bags

Directions:
1. Combine all the ingredients in a slow cooker.
2. Cover and cook for 1 hour on low.
3. Remove the lemon slices and tea bags, then pour into mugs.
4. Serve warm.

Pomegranate Cider

Time: 2 hrs. 15 mins   **Servings: 6**
Ingredients:
1 star anise
1 small orange, sliced
4 cups apple cider
1 1/2 cups pomegranate juiced
1/4 cup brown sugar
1/2 cup ginger ale
1 cinnamon stick

Directions:
1. Combine all the ingredients in your crock pot.
2. Cover and cook for 2 hours on low.
3. Serve warm.

Spiced Lemon Cider Punch

Time: 2 hrs. 15 mins   **Servings: 6**
Ingredients:
1 cup cranberry juice
1/4 cup lemon juice
4 cups apple cider
1/4 cup honey
2 cardamom pods, crushed
1 cup water
1 lemon, sliced

Directions:
1. Mix the cranberry juice, lemon juice, apple cider, water, lemon slices, honey, and cardamom pods in your slow cooker.
2. Cover and cook for 2 hours on low.
3. Serve warm.

Brandied Mulled Wine

Time: 1 hr. 45 mins   **Servings: 8**

Ingredients:
2 whole cloves
2 cardamom pods, crushed
1/4 cup maple syrup
1 cinnamon stick
7 cups dry white wine
1 cup brandy
1 star anise

Directions:
1. Combine all the ingredients in your crock pot.
2. Cover and cook for 1 1/2 hours on low.
3. Serve warm.

Caramel Hot Chocolate

Time: 4 hrs. 15 mins   **Servings: 6**

Ingredients:
1 pinch salt
1 cup dark chocolate chips
1 cup evaporated milk
3/4 cup caramel sauce
4 cups whole milk

Directions:
1. Mix all the ingredients in your slow cooker.
2. Cover and cook for 4 hours on low.
3. Serve hot.

Hot Whiskey Sour

Time: 2 hrs. 15 mins   **Servings: 6**

Ingredients:
1 tablespoon honey
1/2 cup sugar
4 cups water
1 cup whiskey
1/2 cup lemon juice

Directions:
1. Combine the ingredients in your crock pot.
2. Cover and cook for 2 hours on low.
3. Serve warm.

Hot Marmalade Cider

Time: 1 hr. 15 mins   **Servings: 6**

Ingredients:
1 orange, sliced
1/4 cup orange marmalade
5 cups apple cider
1 cup fresh orange juice

Directions:
1. Combine all the ingredients in your crock pot.
2. Cover and cook for 1 hour on high.
3. Serve warm.

Peppermint Hot Chocolate

Time: 1 hr. 45 mins   **Servings: 6**

Ingredients:
1 cup dark chocolate
1 pinch salt
4 cups whole milk
1 cup heavy cream
1 tablespoon cocoa powder
1 teaspoon peppermint extract

Directions:
1. Combine all the ingredients in your slow cooker.
2. Cover and cook for 1 1/2 hours on low.
3. Serve warm.

Spicy Mulled Red Wine

Time: 4 hrs. 15 mins   **Servings: 6**

Ingredients:
1 star anise
2 cardamom pods, crushed
1/2 bay leaf
1/2 cup white sugar
1 cinnamon stick
6 cups red wine
1 teaspoon peppercorns

Directions:
1. Mix all the ingredients in your slow cooker.
2. Cover and cook for 4 hours on low.
3. Serve warm.

Orange Brandy Hot Toddy

Time: 2 hrs. 15 mins   **Servings: 6**

Ingredients:
1 cup brandy
1 cinnamon stick
4 cups brewed black tea
1/2-inch piece of ginger, sliced
2 orange slices
1 cup fresh orange juice
1/4 cup honey

Directions:
1. Mix all the ingredients in your slow cooker.
2. Cover and cook for 2 hours on low.
3. Serve hot.

Lemon-Lime Jasmine Tea

Time: 1 hr. 15 mins   **Servings: 6**

Ingredients:
1 lemon, sliced
1 lime, sliced
6 cups water
1/2 cup sugar
2 tablespoons jasmine buds

Directions:
1. Mix all the ingredients in your crock pot.
2. Cook for 1 hour on high.
3. Serve hot.

Party Cranberry Punch

Time: 4 hrs. 15 mins   **Servings: 6**

Ingredients:
1/2 cup fresh or frozen cranberries
1 small orange, sliced
2 cups cranberry juice
2 tablespoons honey
2 cinnamon sticks
4 cups apple cider
1 red apple, cored and sliced
1 peach, pitted and sliced

Directions:
1. Combine all the ingredients in your crock pot.
2. Cook for 4 hours on low
3. Serve warm.

Caramel Cider

Time: 1 hr. 15 mins   **Servings: 6**

Ingredients:
1 cinnamon stick
1/2 cup water
4 cups apple cider
1/2 cups sugar
1 cup fresh orange juice

Directions:
1. Heat the sugar in a pan until it has an amber color. Add water and cook for 2 minutes, until the sugar is fully dissolved and melted.
2. Mix the caramel sauce with the remaining ingredients in your crock pot.
3. Cook for 1 hour on high.
4. Serve warm.

Hot Cranberry Toddy

Time: 4 hrs. 15 mins   **Servings: 8**

Ingredients:
1/2 cup fresh or frozen cranberries
1/4 cup dark rum
1/4 cup light brown sugar
6 cups apple cider
2 cups cranberry juice

Directions:
1. Combine all the ingredients in your crock pot.
2. Cook for 4 hours on low.
3. Serve warm.

The Ultimate Hot Chocolate

Time: 4 hrs. 15 mins   **Servings: 6**

Ingredients:
1 pinch salt
1 cup sweetened condensed milk
1 cup heavy cream
1 cup dark chocolate chips
4 cups whole milk
1 tablespoon cocoa powder
Mini marshmallows for serving

Directions:
1. Combine all the ingredients except marshmallows in your crock pot.
2. Cover and cook for 4 hours on low.
3. Serve hot, topped with marshmallows.

Buttered Hot Rum

Time: 4 hrs. 15 mins   **Servings: 6**

Ingredients:
1/4 cup butter
1 cup dark rum
2 cinnamon stick
4 cups water
1 cup dark brown sugar
1 whole clove

Directions:
1. Combine the butter, cinnamon, water, sugar, and whole clove in your slow cooker.
2. Cook for 4 hours on low.
3. Add the rum and serve immediately.

Irish Cream Coffee

Time: 3 hrs. 15 mins   **Servings: 4**

Ingredients
1/2 cup heavy cream
1 tablespoon cocoa powder
3 cups brewed coffee
1/2 cup Irish cream liqueur

Directions:
1. Combine all the ingredients in your crockpot.
2. Cook for 3 hours on low.
3. Serve warm.

CHAPTER 7

PORK RECIPES

Brazilian Pork Stew

Time: 7 hrs. 15 mins   **Servings: 6**

Ingredients:

2 sweet onions, chopped
4 bacon slices, chopped
1/2 pound dried black beans
1 1/2 pounds pork shoulder, cubed
2 cups chicken stock
Salt and pepper
2 bay leaves
1 teaspoon white wine vinegar
1/2 teaspoon ground coriander
4 garlic cloves, chopped
1 teaspoon cumin seeds

Directions:

1. Mix the beans and pork with the remaining ingredients in your crock pot.
2. Add salt and pepper and cover.
3. Cook on low for 7 hours.
4. Serve warm.

Apple Bourbon Pork Chops

Time: 8 hrs. 15 mins   **Servings: 6**

Ingredients:

1 thyme sprig
1 rosemary sprig
6 pork chops
1/4 cup bourbon
1/2 cup chicken stock
4 red apples, cored and sliced
1/2 cup applesauce
Salt and pepper

Directions:

1. Mix the pork chops with salt and pepper.
2. Put the apples, applesauce, bourbon, stock, thyme and rosemary in your slow cooker.
3. Place the pork chops on top and cook on low for 8 hours.
4. Serve the pork chops topped with sauce.

BBQ Pork Ribs

Time: 11 hrs. 15 mins   **Servings: 8**

Ingredients:

1 celery stalk, sliced
1 tablespoon Dijon mustard
1 teaspoon chili powder
1/4 cup chicken stock
Salt and pepper
5 pounds pork short ribs
2 cups BBQ sauce
1 large onion, sliced
1 tablespoon brown sugar
4 garlic cloves, minced

Directions:

1. Place all ingredients in your slow cooker.
2. Add salt and pepper and cook on low for 11 hours.
3. Serve warm.

Red Wine Braised Pork Ribs

Time: 8 hrs. 15 mins   **Servings: 8**

Ingredients:

1 teaspoon chili powder
1 teaspoon cumin powder
1 tablespoon molasses
1 teaspoon salt
1 cup BBQ sauce
2 tablespoons olive oil
1 teaspoon dried thyme
5 pounds pork short ribs
4 tablespoons brown sugar
1 cup red wine

Directions:

1. Combine the brown sugar, molasses, olive oil, chili powder, cumin powder, thyme and salt in a bowl.
2. Spread this mixture over the pork ribs, coating the meat well.
3. Put it in your crock pot.
4. Add the BBQ sauce and red wine and cook on low for 8 hours.
5. Serve warm.

Onion Pork Tenderloin

Time: 8 hrs. 15 mins   **Servings: 6**

Ingredients:
1/2 cup chicken stock
Salt and pepper
1 thyme sprig
2 tablespoons canola oil
3 large sweet onions, sliced
2 pounds pork tenderloin
6 bacon slices
1/2 cup white wine

Directions:
1. Heat the oil in a pan and add the onions. Cook for 10 minutes until softened and a little bit caramelized.
2. Place the onions in your crock pot and add the remaining ingredients.
3. Add salt and pepper and cook on low for 8 hours.

Fennel–Infused Ham

Time: 6 hrs. 15 mins   **Servings: 8**

Ingredients:
1 orange, zested and juiced
1/2 cup white wine
4-5 pounds ham
1 thyme sprig
Salt and pepper
2 fennel bulbs, sliced
1 cup chicken stock
2 bay leaves

Directions:
1. Mix the fennel, orange zest, orange juice, white wine, chicken stock, bay leaves and thyme in your crock pot.
2. Add salt and pepper and place the ham on top.
3. Cook on low for 6 hours.
4. Serve warm.

Country Style Pork Ribs

Time: 6 hrs. 15 mins   **Servings: 4**

Ingredients:
1 teaspoon garlic powder
1 cup pineapple juice
1 tablespoon brown sugar
3 pounds short pork ribs
1 teaspoon salt
1 teaspoon dried thyme

Directions:
1. Sprinkle the pork ribs with salt, garlic powder, brown sugar and thyme and place into your slow cooker.
2. Add the pineapple juice and cook on low for 6 hours.
3. Serve warm.

Chili Verde

Time: 7 hrs. 15 mins   **Servings: 8**

Ingredients:
1 teaspoon dried oregano
1 teaspoon cumin powder
1 large onion, chopped
4 garlic cloves, chopped
1/2 teaspoon smoked paprika
2 green chilis, chopped
1/4 teaspoon chili powder
1 bunch cilantro, chopped
1 1/2 cups chicken stock
Salt and pepper
2 pounds pork shoulder, cubed
2 tablespoons canola oil
2 pounds tomatillos, peeled and chopped

Directions:
1. Heat the oil in a pan and add the pork shoulder. Cook for a few minutes until golden, then place it in your slow cooker.
2. Add the remaining ingredients and sprinkle with salt and pepper.
3. Cook on low for 7 hours.
4. Serve warm.

Mexican Pork Roast

Time: 8 hrs. 15 mins   **Servings: 6**
Ingredients:
1 bay leaf
1 cup chicken stock
Salt and pepper
2 carrots, sliced
2 celery stalks, sliced
2 pounds pork shoulder, cubed
1 teaspoon smoked paprika
1/2 teaspoon cumin powder
1 can fire roasted tomatoes
1 large onion, chopped

Directions:
1. Mix the pork shoulder, tomatoes, carrots, celery, onion, paprika, cumin powder, bay leaf, stock, salt and pepper.
2. Cook on low for 8 hours.
3. Serve warm.

Balsamic Roasted Pork

Time: 6 hrs. 15 mins   **Servings: 8**
Ingredients:
1 teaspoon five-spice powder
1 teaspoon hot sauce
1/4 cup balsamic vinegar
1 teaspoon garlic powder
2 tablespoons honey
Salt and pepper
4 pounds pork shoulder, cubed
2 tablespoons brown sugar

Directions:
1. Combine the sugar, five-spice powder, honey and hot sauce in a bowl. Pour the mixture over the pork.
2. Place the pork in the crock pot and add the vinegar.
3. Add salt and pepper and cook on low for 6 hours.
4. Serve warm with your favorite side dish.

Pineapple Cranberry Ham

Time: 7 hrs. 15 mins   **Servings: 6**
Ingredients:
1 bay leaf
1 star anise
Salt and pepper
1 cup pineapple juice
1/2 teaspoon chili powder
2-3 pounds smoked ham
1 cup cranberry sauce
1/2 teaspoon cumin powder
1 cinnamon stick

Directions:
1. Combine the cranberry sauce, pineapple juice, chili powder, cumin powder, cinnamon, star anise, and bay leaf in a crock pot.
2. Place the ham in the crock pot and add salt and pepper if needed.
3. Cook on low for 7 hours.
4. Serve warm with your favorite side dish.

Italian Style Pork Shoulder

Time: 7 hrs. 15 mins   **Servings: 6**
Ingredients:
4 garlic cloves, chopped
2 celery stalks, sliced
2 pounds pork shoulder
1/4 cup white wine
Salt and pepper
1 teaspoon dried thyme
1 teaspoon dried basil
1 thyme sprig
1 large onion, sliced
2 ripe tomatoes, peeled and diced

Directions:
1. Mix all the ingredients in your crock pot and add enough salt and pepper.
2. Cover and cook on low for 7 hours.
3. Serve warm with your favorite side dish.

Apple Butter Short Ribs

Time: 8 hrs. 15 mins   **Servings: 8**

Ingredients:
2 tablespoons brown sugar
1 teaspoon garlic powder
Salt and pepper
1/2 teaspoon chili powder
1/2 cup BBQ sauce
1 cup vegetable stock
4 pounds pork short ribs
1 cup apple butter
1 teaspoon onion powder

Directions:
1. Combine the apple butter, sugar, garlic powder, onion powder, chili powder, BBQ sauce and stock in your slow cooker.
2. Add the ribs, salt, and pepper.
3. Cover and cook on low for 8 hours.
4. Serve warm.

Ginger Beer Pork Ribs

Time: 6 hrs. 45 mins   **Servings: 6**

Ingredients:
1/2 cup ketchup
Salt and pepper
1 tablespoon Worcestershire sauce
2-3 pounds pork short ribs
1/2 teaspoon smoked paprika
1 tablespoon brown sugar
1 cup ginger beer
1 tablespoon Dijon mustard

Directions:
1. Put all the ingredients in your crock pot.
2. Add salt and pepper.
3. Cook on low for 6 1/2 hours.
4. Serve warm with your favorite side dish.

Teriyaki Pork Tenderloin

Time: 7 hrs. 15 mins   **Servings: 6**

Ingredients:
1/4 cup ketchup
1 onion, chopped
2 pounds pork tenderloin
1/4 cup soy sauce
1 tablespoon hot sauce
1/4 cup chicken stock or water
4 garlic cloves, minced
1 tablespoon smooth peanut butter
1 tablespoon brown sugar

Directions:
1. Place the soy sauce, ketchup, onion, peanut butter, sugar, hot sauce, garlic and stock in your crock pot.
2. Add the pork tenderloin.
3. Cook on low for 7 hours.
4. Serve warm with your favorite side dish.

Sauerkraut Cumin Pork

Time: 6 hrs. 15 mins   **Servings: 6**

Ingredients:
1 large onion, chopped
2 carrots, grated
1 1/2 pounds pork shoulder, cubed
1 1/2 pounds sauerkraut, shredded
1 cup chicken stock
1 bay leaf
1 1/2 teaspoons cumin seeds
1/4 teaspoon red pepper flakes
Salt and pepper

Directions:
1. Put all the ingredients in your crock pot.
2. Add salt and pepper
3. Cook on low for 6 hours.
4. Serve warm.

Herbed Roasted Pork

Time: 6 hrs. 15 mins   **Servings: 6**

Ingredients:
1/2 cup chopped cilantro
4 basil leaves
1/2 cup grated Parmesan
Salt and pepper
1 lemon, juiced
2 pounds pork tenderloin
1 cup chopped parsley
1/4 cup pine nuts
1/2 cup chicken stock

Directions:
1. Combine the parsley, cilantro, basil, pine nuts, stock, Parmesan cheese, lemon juice, salt and pepper in a food processor and blend until smooth.
2. Mix the pork tenderloin with the herb mixture and cook on low for 6 hours.
3. Serve with your favorite side dish.

Chili BBQ Ribs

Time: 8 hrs. 30 mins   **Servings: 8**

Ingredients:
1 1/2 teaspoons chili powder
1 teaspoon cumin powder
6 pounds pork short ribs
2 cups BBQ sauce
1 teaspoon Worcestershire sauce
2 tablespoons brown sugar
2 tablespoons red wine vinegar
Salt and pepper

Directions:
1. Combine the BBQ sauce, chili powder, sugar, vinegar, Worcestershire sauce, salt, and pepper in a slow cooker.
2. Add the short ribs and stir until well coated.
3. Cover and cook on low for 8 1/4 hours.
4. Serve warm.

Lemon Roasted Pork Tenderloin

Time: 7 hrs. 15 mins   **Servings: 6**

Ingredients:
Salt and pepper
1 teaspoon black pepper kernels
1 cup canola oil
2 pounds pork tenderloin
1 lemon, sliced
1 cup vegetable stock

Directions:
1. Mix all the ingredients in your slow cooker.
2. Add salt and pepper and cook on low for 7 hours.
3. Serve warm.

Sour Cream Pork Chops

Time: 6 hrs. 15 mins   **Servings: 6**

Ingredients:
1/2 cup chicken stock
Salt and pepper
2 green onions, chopped
6 pork chops, bone in
1 cup sour cream
2 tablespoons chopped parsley

Directions:
1. Place the pork chops, sour cream, stock, onions and parsley in your crock pot.
2. Add salt and pepper and cook on low for 6 hours.
3. Serve warm, topped with plenty of sauce.

Hawaiian Pork Roast

Time: 8 hrs. 15 mins   **Servings: 8**
Ingredients:
1 rosemary sprig
1 bay leaf
Salt and pepper
1 cup pineapple juice
1 cup frozen cranberries
4 pounds pork roast
1 mango, peeled and cubed
2 tablespoons red wine vinegar

Directions:
1. Place the pork roast, mango cubes, pineapple juice, cranberries, vinegar, bay leaf and rosemary sprig in the slow cooker.
2. Add salt and pepper
3. Cook on low for 8 hours.
4. Serve warm.

Black Bean Pork Stew

Time: 9 hrs. 15 mins   **Servings: 10**
Ingredients:
1 pound dried black beans
1 can fire roasted tomatoes
2 red onions, chopped
4 garlic cloves, chopped
1 teaspoon dried oregano
1 teaspoon dried basil
1 teaspoon cumin powder
3 pounds pork roast, cubed
Salt and pepper
1 teaspoon chili powder
2 cups chicken stock
2 chipotle peppers, chopped

Directions:
1. Put the onions, garlic, black beans, tomatoes, stock, chipotle peppers, oregano, basil, cumin powder, chili powder and pork roast in a slow cooker.
2. Add salt and pepper
3. Cook on low for 9 hours.
4. Serve warm and fresh or chilled.

Honey Glazed Pork Ribs

Time: 8 hrs. 15 mins   **Servings: 6**
Ingredients:
2 tablespoons honey
1 star anise
1/4 cup BBQ sauce
1 tablespoon maple syrup
1 cup chicken stock
1 teaspoon salt
4 pounds pork ribs
2 tablespoons honey mustard
1/2 teaspoon cayenne pepper

Directions:
1. Put the mustard, honey, maple syrup, star anise, BBQ sauce, stock, salt and cayenne pepper in your slow cooker.
2. Add the pork ribs and coat them with sauce.
3. Cover and cook on low for 8 hours.
4. Serve warm.

Mango Flavored Pulled Pork

Time: 7 hrs. 15 mins   **Servings: 8**
Ingredients:
1 tablespoon balsamic vinegar
1 cup BBQ sauce
1 cup chicken stock
1 chipotle pepper, chopped
1 ripe mango, peeled and diced
1/4 cup bourbon
Salt and pepper
4 pounds pork roast, cut into large pieces

Directions:
1. Put all the ingredients in your crock pot.
2. Add salt and pepper to taste and cook on low for 7 hours.
3. Serve warm.

Pork Sausage Stew

Time: 6 hrs. 15 mins   **Servings: 8**
Ingredients:
2 carrots, diced
1 celery stalk, diced
1 cup red lentils
2/3 cup brown lentils
1 bay leaf
1 chipotle pepper, chopped
Salt and pepper
1 cup diced tomatoes
2 garlic cloves, chopped
1-pound fresh pork sausages, sliced
1 large onion, finely chopped
1 tablespoon tomato paste
3 cups chicken stock
2 tablespoons chopped parsley for serving

Directions:
1. Place all ingredients except parsley in the slow cooker.
2. Add salt and pepper to taste.
3. Cook on low for 6 hours.
4. Serve warm, topped with chopped parsley.

Sweet Potato Pork Stew

Time: 6 hrs. 15 mins   **Servings: 6**
Ingredients:
2 shallots, chopped
Salt and pepper
2 red apples, peeled and cubed
1 pinch nutmeg
2 tablespoons tomato paste
2 cups chicken stock
1 teaspoon Dijon mustard
1 1/2 pounds pork tenderloin, cubed
3 large sweet potatoes, peeled and cubed

Directions:
1. Put the pork, sweet potatoes, shallots, apples, nutmeg, mustard, tomato paste and stock in your slow cooker.
2. Add salt and pepper
3. Cook on low for 6 hours.
4. Serve warm or re-heated.

Roasted Bell Pepper Pork Stew

Time: 5 hrs. 15 mins   **Servings: 6**
Ingredients:
1 cup chicken stock
1 cup tomato sauce
Salt and pepper
1 jar roasted bell pepper, drained and chopped
4 garlic cloves, chopped
1 large onion, chopped
1/2 teaspoon red pepper flakes
2 pounds pork tenderloin, cubed
2 tablespoons canola oil

Directions:
1. Heat the oil in a pan and add the pork. Cook for a few minutes until golden. Place it in your slow cooker.
2. Add the remaining ingredients and sprinkle with salt and pepper.
3. Cover and cook on low for 5 hours.
4. Serve warm.

Red Chili Pulled Pork

Time: 7 hrs. 15 mins   **Servings: 8**
Ingredients:
Salt and pepper
2 red chilis, seeded and chopped
1 large onion, chopped
4 pounds pork roast
1 cup tomato sauce
1 cup red salsa

Directions:
1. Mix all the ingredients in your slow cooker.
2. Add salt and pepper.
3. Cook on low for 7 hours.
4. When done, shred the pork into fine threads using two forks.
5. Serve warm.

Blackberry Pork Tenderloin

Time: 7 hrs. 15 mins   **Servings: 6**

Ingredients:
2 red onions, sliced
1/2 cup chicken stock
Salt and pepper
1/2 teaspoon dried sage
1/2 teaspoon dried oregano
2 tablespoons honey
2 pounds pork tenderloin
2 cups fresh blackberries
1 tablespoon balsamic vinegar

Directions:
1. Mix all the ingredients in your crock pot.
2. Add salt and pepper and cover.
3. Cook on low for 7 hours.
4. When done, slice the pork and serve warm.

Havana Style Pork Roast

Time: 6 hrs. 15 mins   **Servings: 6**

Ingredients:
1 celery stalk, sliced
4 garlic cloves, chopped
2 pounds pork roast
1 onion, sliced
1/2 cup fresh orange juice
1/4 teaspoon chili powder
1 bay leaf
Salt and pepper
1 lemon, zested and juiced
1 teaspoon cumin powder

Directions:
1. Mix all the ingredients in your slow cooker.
2. Add salt and pepper and cook on low for 6 hours.
3. Serve warm.

Creamy Dijon Pork Shoulder

Time: 7 hrs. 15 mins   **Servings: 8**

Ingredients:
4 garlic cloves, chopped
1 large onion, chopped
2 tablespoons canola oil
4 pounds pork tenderloin
2 cups sliced mushrooms
1 can condensed cream of mushroom soup
Salt and pepper
2 tablespoons Dijon mustard

Directions:
1. Heat the canola oil in a pan. Sprinkle the pork with salt and pepper, then fry in the hot oil.
2. Place the meat in your slow cooker.
3. Add the remaining ingredients and sprinkle with additional salt and pepper.
4. Cook on low for 7 hours.
5. Serve the pork warm, topped with the creamy sauce.

Marsala Pork Chops

Time: 6 hrs. 15 mins   **Servings: 6**

Ingredients:
6 pork chops
2 tablespoons all-purpose flour
1 teaspoon garlic powder
1 onion, sliced
4 garlic cloves, chopped
2 cups sliced mushrooms
1/2 cup Marsala wine
1 can condensed cream of mushroom soup
Salt and pepper

Directions:
1. Sprinkle the pork chops with salt and pepper, then coat with flour.
2. Place the pork chops in your slow cooker and add the remaining ingredients.
3. Sprinkle with salt and pepper.
4. Cook on low for 6 hours.
5. Serve the pork chops warm, topped with sauce.

Slow-Cooked Pork in Tomato Sauce

Time: 8 hrs. 15 mins   **Servings: 8**
Ingredients:
Salt and pepper
2 tablespoons tomato paste
1 teaspoon cumin seeds
1 teaspoon fennel seeds
1 teaspoon garlic powder
2 bay leaves
4 pounds pork tenderloin
2 cups tomato sauce
1 teaspoon celery seeds
Directions:
1. Mix all the ingredients in your slow cooker.
2. Add salt and pepper
3. Cook the pork on low for 8 hours.
4. Serve warm with your favorite side dish.

Sweet and Sour Pork Chops

Time: 3 hrs. 15 mins   **Servings: 6**
Ingredients:
1/4 teaspoon cumin seeds
Salt and pepper
2 garlic cloves, chopped
1 celery stalk, sliced
1 cup apple cider
6 pork chops
1 large onion, sliced
2 tablespoons balsamic vinegar
2 tablespoons honey
1 bay leaf

Directions:
1. Mix the onion, garlic, celery, vinegar, honey, cider, cumin seeds and bay leaf in a crock pot.
2. Mix the pork chops with salt and pepper and place them in the crock pot.
3. Cook on high for 3 hours.
4. Serve warm.

Tomato Sauce Pork Roast

Time: 3 hrs. 15 mins   **Servings: 4**
Ingredients:
1/4 teaspoon cayenne pepper
Salt and pepper
1/2 cup tomato sauce
1/2 cup chicken stock
2 pounds pork roast, cubed
2 tablespoons canola oil
2 tablespoons tomato paste

Directions:
1. Combine all the ingredients in your slow cooker.
2. Add salt and pepper and cook on high for 3 hours.
3. Serve warm and fresh with your favorite side dish.

Bacon Potato Stew

Time: 6 hrs. 30 mins   **Servings: 6**
Ingredients:
2 carrots, diced
1 celery stalk, diced
2 sweet potatoes, peeled and cubed
1 pound Yukon gold potatoes, peeled and cubed
2 red bell peppers, cored and diced
1/2 teaspoon chili powder
1 cup diced tomatoes
Salt and pepper
1 cup diced bacon
1 large onion, chopped
1/2 teaspoon cumin seeds
2 cups chicken stock

Directions:
1. Heat a pan and add the bacon. Cook until crisp, then place in the slow cooker.
2. Add the remaining ingredients and salt and pepper.
3. Cook on low for 6 hours.
4. Serve warm.

Miso Braised Pork

Time: 7 hrs. 15 mins   **Servings: 8**
Ingredients:
1 tablespoon grated ginger
1 cup vegetable stock
1 lemongrass stalk, crushed
2 tablespoons canola oil
4 pounds pork shoulder
6 garlic cloves, minced
2 tablespoons miso paste

Directions:
1. Combine the garlic, ginger, canola oil, miso paste, stock and lemongrass in your crock pot.
2. Put the pork shoulder in the crock pot and cover.
3. Cook on low for 7 hours.
4. Serve warm with your favorite side dish.

Red Bean Pork Stew

Time: 3 hrs. 15 mins   **Servings: 6**
Ingredients:
1 chorizo link, sliced
1 red onion, chopped
1 teaspoon hot sauce
4 bacon slices, chopped
4 garlic cloves, chopped
Salt and pepper
1 bay leaf
1 can fire roasted tomatoes
2 cups vegetable stock
1/2 pound dried red beans, rinsed
1 1/2 pounds pork roast, cubed

Directions:
1. Place the beans, pork roast, chorizo, bacon, garlic, onion and hot sauce in your slow cooker.
2. Add the tomatoes, stock, bay leaf, salt and pepper.
3. Cook on high for 3 hours.
4. Serve warm.

Smoked Ham and Lima Bean Stew

Time: 6 hrs. 15 mins   **Servings: 6**
Ingredients:
Salt and pepper
2 cups water
1 cup chicken stock
2 cups diced smoked ham
1 pound dried lima beans
1/4 teaspoon garlic powder
1/4 teaspoon onion powder
1 cup diced tomatoes
1 teaspoon Cajun seasoning
1/4 teaspoon cayenne pepper

Directions:
1. Combine all ingredients in your slow cooker.
2. Cook on low for 6 hours.
3. Serve warm.

Spiced Plum Pork Chops

Time: 7 hrs. 15 mins   **Servings: 6**
Ingredients:
1/2 cup apple cider
2 tablespoons brown sugar
1 star anise
1 bay leaf
2 whole cloves
Salt and pepper
1/2 cup chicken stock
6 pork chops
6 plums, pitted and chopped
1 tablespoon balsamic vinegar
1 cinnamon stick

Directions:
1. Combine the plums, apple cider, stock, vinegar, brown sugar, star anise, cinnamon, bay leaf, and cloves in the crock pot.
2. Add the pork chops, then season with salt and pepper.
3. Cook on low for 7 hours.
4. Serve warm.

Green Enchilada Pork Roast

Time: 8 hrs. 15 mins   **Servings: 8**
Ingredients:
1/2 cup vegetable stock
Salt and pepper
1/2 cup chopped cilantro
4 pounds pork roast
2 cups green enchilada sauce
2 chipotle peppers, chopped

Directions:
1. Place the enchilada sauce, cilantro, chipotle peppers and stock in your slow cooker.
2. Add the pork roast and also salt and pepper.
3. Cook on low for 8 hours.
4. Serve warm with your favorite side dish.

Navy Bean Stew

Time: 10 hrs. 15 mins   **Servings: 10**
Ingredients:
1 cup chicken stock
Salt and pepper
1 pound dried navy beans, rinsed
1 cup dried red beans, rinsed
2 celery stalks, sliced
2 carrots, sliced
2 large onions, chopped
4 pounds pork shoulder, cubed
1/2 cup diced bacon
1 can fire roasted tomatoes
2 chipotle peppers, chopped

Directions:
1. Combine all ingredients in your crock pot.
2. Add salt and pepper.
3. Cook on low for 10 hours.
4. Serve warm.

Ham Scalloped Potatoes

Time: 6 hrs. 30 mins   **Servings: 8**
Ingredients:
1 large onion, sliced
Salt and pepper
2 cups grated Cheddar cheese
2 cups whole milk
1 tablespoon all-purpose flour
2 pounds potatoes, peeled and finely sliced
1/2 pound smoked ham, finely sliced
1 cup heavy cream

Directions:
1. Place the potatoes, ham and onion in your slow cooker.
2. Combine the milk, flour, and cream in a bowl. Add salt and pepper, then pour over the potatoes.
3. Cover and cook on low for 6 hours.
4. Serve warm.

Ginger Slow-Roasted Pork

Time: 7 hrs. 15 mins   **Servings: 8**
Ingredients:
Salt and pepper
1 tablespoon soy sauce
1 tablespoon honey
4 pounds pork shoulder
2 teaspoons grated ginger
1 1/2 cups vegetable stock

Directions:
1. Rub the pork shoulder with salt and pepper, then top with ginger, soy sauce and honey.
2. Put the pork in your slow cooker and add the stock.
3. Cover and cook on low for 7 hours.
4. Serve warm with your favorite side dish.

Smoky Pork Chili

Time: 6 hrs. 15 mins   **Servings: 8**

Ingredients:
1 teaspoon cumin powder
1 pound ground pork
Salt and pepper
2 tablespoon tomato paste
1 cup dark beer
2 bay leaves
1 thyme sprig
2 onions, chopped
1 pound dried black beans, rinsed
2 1/2 cups vegetable stock
1 cup diced tomatoes
4 garlic cloves, chopped
1 tablespoon canola oil
6 bacon slices, chopped
1 1/2 teaspoons smoked paprika

Directions:
1. Heat the oil in a pan and add the bacon. Cook until crisp, then add the pork. Cook for a few additional minutes then transfer to your slow cooker.
2. Add the remaining ingredients and season with salt and pepper.
3. Cook on low for 6 hours.
4. Serve warm.

Curried Roasted Pork

Time: 6 hrs. 15 mins   **Servings: 6**

Ingredients:
Salt and pepper
1 cup coconut milk
1/2 teaspoon chili powder
4 garlic cloves, minced
2 pounds pork roast
1 1/2 teaspoons curry powder
1 teaspoon dried mint
1 teaspoon dried basil

Directions:
1. Sprinkle the pork roast with salt, pepper, curry powder, chili powder, garlic, mint, basil, salt and pepper.
2. Put the meat in your crock pot and add the coconut milk.
3. Cover and cook on low for 6 hours.
4. Serve warm.

Asian Style Pot Roast

Time: 6 hrs. 15 mins   **Servings: 8**

Ingredients:
4 garlic cloves, minced
2 shallots, sliced
1 cup chicken stock
1 pound baby carrots
4 potatoes, peeled and halved
Salt and pepper
1/4 cup low sodium soy sauce
2 tablespoons tomato paste
1 tablespoon hot sauce
1/2 lemongrass stalk, crushed
4 pounds boneless chuck roast, trimmed and halved

Directions:
1. Combine all ingredients in the crock pot.
2. Add salt and pepper.
3. Cook on low for 6 hours.
4. Serve warm.

French Onion Roasted Pork Chops

Time: 6 hrs. 15 mins   **Servings: 6**

Ingredients:
1 can condensed onion soup
1 teaspoon garlic powder
6 pork chops
1/4 cup white wine
Salt and pepper

Directions:
1. Mix all the ingredients in your slow cooker.
2. Add salt and pepper and cover.
3. Cook on low for 6 hours.
4. Serve warm.

Cuban Pork Chops

Time: 6 hrs. 15 mins   **Servings: 6**
Ingredients:
1 teaspoon grated ginger
1 bay leaf
Salt and pepper
4 garlic cloves, chopped
1 teaspoon chili powder
1 teaspoon cumin seeds
6 pork chops
2 large onions, sliced
1 lemon, juiced
1 cup chicken stock

Directions:
1. Combine all the ingredients in your slow cooker and add salt and pepper.
2. Cover and cook on low for 6 hours.
3. Serve warm.

Red Beans and Rice

Time: 3 hrs. 15 mins   **Servings: 6**
Ingredients:
1 tablespoon canola oil
1 red onion, chopped
1 1/2 cups chicken stock
Salt and pepper
1 lemon for serving
1 cup green peas
1 can (15 oz. red beans, drained
1 pounds ground pork
1 chorizo link, chopped
1/2 cup frozen sweet corn
1/2 cup wild rice
Directions:
1. Heat the canola oil in a pan and add the pork. Cook for a few minutes then place in your crock pot.
2. Add the remaining ingredients and also salt and pepper.
3. Cook on high for 3 hours until the rice absorbs all the water.
4. Before serving the dish, drizzle in the lemon juice and stir well. Serve warm.

Thyme-Flavored White Bean Pork Cassoulet

Time: 4 hrs. 15 mins   **Servings: 4**
Ingredients:
Salt and pepper
1 can (15 oz.) white beans, drained
2 thyme sprigs
1 cup chicken stock
1 garlic clove, chopped
1 celery stalk, sliced
1 shallot, chopped
1 cup diced tomatoes
1 pound pork tenderloin, cubed
2 tablespoons canola oil

Directions:
1. Heat the oil in a pan and add the pork. Cook for a few minutes until golden brown then place in your slow cooker.
2. Add the remaining ingredients in a slow cooker and add salt and pepper.
3. Cook on low for 4 hours and serve it warm.

Apricot-Glazed Ham

Time: 6 hrs. 15 mins   **Servings: 6-8**
Ingredients:
1 teaspoon cumin powder
1/4 teaspoon chili powder
3-4 pounds ham
1/2 cup apricot preserves
Salt and pepper
1 cup vegetable stock

Directions:
1. Combine the apricot preserves with cumin powder and chili powder, then spread over the ham.
2. Put the meat in your slow cooker and add the stock.
3. Cook on low for 6 hours.
4. Serve warm with your favorite side dish.

Pork Chickpea Stew

Time: 2 hrs. 15 mins   **Servings: 6**

Ingredients:
2 celery stalks, sliced
2 carrots, sliced
1 pound pork roast, cubed
2 tablespoons canola oil
1 thyme sprig
Salt and pepper
1 can (15 oz.) chickpeas, drained
1 cup chicken stock
2 red bell peppers, cored and diced
1 can fire roasted tomatoes
1 bay leaf

Directions:
1. Heat the oil in a pan and add the pork. Cook until golden, then transfer to your crock pot.
2. Add the remaining ingredients and season with salt and pepper.
3. Cook on high for 2 hours.
4. Serve warm.

Veggie Medley Roasted Pork Tenderloin

Time: 7 hrs. 15 mins   **Servings: 6**

Ingredients:
2 carrots, sliced
1 shallot
2 1/2 pounds pork tenderloin
1 cup chicken stock
Salt and pepper
2 ripe heirloom tomatoes, peeled
4 garlic cloves
1 cup cauliflower florets

Directions:
1. Mix the tomatoes, carrots, shallot, garlic, cauliflower, stock, salt and pepper in your blender.
2. Blend until smooth, then mix it with the pork tenderloin in your crock pot.
3. Cover and cook on low for 7 hours.
4. Serve warm.

Spiced Pork Belly

Time: 7 hrs. 15 mins   **Servings: 6**

Ingredients:
1 tablespoon brown sugar
1 teaspoon chili powder
3 pounds pork belly
1 tablespoon cumin powder
1 teaspoon grated ginger
1 tablespoon soy sauce
1 tablespoon molasses
2 garlic cloves, minced
1/2 cup white wine

Directions:
1. Combine the cumin powder, sugar, chili powder, ginger, molasses, garlic and soy sauce in a bowl.
2. Spread this mixture over the pork belly and rub it well into the skin and meat.
3. Put the belly in your crock pot and add the wine.
4. Cook on low for 7 hours.
5. Serve warm with your favorite side dish.

Peanut Butter Pork Belly

Time: 6 hrs. 15 mins   **Servings: 6**

Ingredients:
2 tablespoons soy sauce
1 teaspoon grated ginger
1 tablespoon honey
4 garlic cloves
1 chipotle pepper, chopped
1 tablespoon hot sauce
1/2 cup vegetable stock
3 pounds pork belly
1/4 cup smooth peanut butter

Directions:
1. Combine the peanut butter, soy sauce, hot sauce, stock, garlic, ginger, honey and chipotle pepper in a crock pot.
2. Add the pork belly and mix.
3. Cover and cook on low for 6 hours.
4. Serve warm.

Lemon Vegetable Pork Roast

Time: 8 hrs. 15 mins   **Servings: 8**
Ingredients:
1/4 teaspoon cayenne pepper
Salt and pepper
1 lemon, sliced
1/2 pounds baby carrots
1 cup vegetable stock
1 tablespoon molasses
2 large potatoes, peeled and cubed
2 tablespoons soy sauce
2 tablespoon ketchup
1/4 cup red wine vinegar
2 cups snap peas
1 large onion, sliced
4 pounds pork roast, cut into quarters
2 parsnips, sliced
1 teaspoon garlic powder

Directions:
1. Mix the onion, pork roast, baby carrots, snap peas, parsnips, potatoes, stock, molasses, vinegar, soy sauce, ketchup, garlic powder and cayenne pepper in your slow cooker.
2. Add salt and pepper and cover with lemon slices.
3. Cook on low for 8 hours.
4. Serve warm.

Hearty BBQ Pork Belly

Time: 7 hrs. 15 mins   **Servings: 8**
Ingredients:
2 chipotle peppers, chopped
1 teaspoon salt
1 thyme sprig
2 red onions, sliced
4 pounds pork belly, trimmed
2 cups BBQ sauce
6 garlic cloves, chopped

Directions:
1. Mix all the ingredients in your slow cooker.
2. Cover and cook on low for 7 hours.
3. Serve warm with your favorite side dish.

Pork Belly over Smoky Sauerkraut

Time: 8 hrs. 30 mins   **Servings: 8**
Ingredients:
1 cup chicken stock
4 pounds pork belly
Salt and pepper
1 teaspoon smoked paprika
1 teaspoon cumin seeds
1 pound sauerkraut, chopped
6 bacon slices, chopped
1/2 teaspoon dried thyme

Directions:
1. Combine the sauerkraut, bacon, paprika, cumin seeds, thyme and stock in your crock pot.
2. Add salt and pepper and place it over the sauerkraut.
3. Cover and cook on low for 8 hours.
4. Serve warm.

Red Cabbage Pork Stew

Time: 4 hrs. 15 mins   **Servings: 6**
Ingredients:
2 tablespoons canola oil
4 garlic cloves, minced
1 tablespoon maple syrup
1/4 cup apple cider vinegar
Salt and pepper
1 large onion, chopped
1 head red cabbage, shredded
1 1/2 pounds pork roast, cubed
1 teaspoon chili powder

Directions:
1. Mix all the ingredients in your crock pot.
2. Add salt and pepper
3. Cook on low for 4 hours.
4. Serve warm.

Cheddar Pork Casserole

Time: 5 hrs. 30 mins **Servings: 6**
Ingredients:
Salt and pepper
2 cups grated cheddar cheese
1 1/2 pounds ground pork
1 cup finely chopped mushrooms
1/2 cup spicy ketchup
1 carrot, grated
2 tablespoons canola oil
2 large onions, sliced

Directions:
1. Heat the canola oil in a pan and add the onions. Cook on low heat for 10 minutes, until they begin to caramelize.
2. Put the onions in your slow cooker. Add the pork, carrot, mushrooms and ketchup and mix well. Add salt and pepper.
3. Top with cheddar cheese and cook on low for 5 hours.
4. Serve warm.

Vietnamese-Style Pork

Time: 7 hrs. 15 mins **Servings: 6**
Ingredients:
6 garlic cloves, minced
1/4 cup brown sugar
2 tablespoons white wine vinegar
1 hot red pepper, chopped
1/2 cup vegetable stock or water
1/2 cup soy sauce
2 pounds pork shoulder
1 teaspoon grated ginger

Directions:
1. Mix all the ingredients in your crock pot.
2. Cover and cook on low for 7 hours.
3. Serve warm.

Mushroom Pork Stew

Time: 5 hrs. 15 mins **Servings: 6**
Ingredients:
1 pound button mushrooms
1 1/2 cups chicken stock
1 pound pork roast, cubed
2 tablespoons canola oil
1 thyme sprig
Salt and pepper
1 tablespoon cornstarch
1 cup cream cheese

Directions:
1. Heat the oil in a pan and add the pork. Cook until golden, then place in your crock pot.
2. Add the remaining ingredients and season with salt and pepper.
3. Cook on low for 5 hours and serve warm.

Golden Maple-Glazed Pork Chops

Time: 4 hrs. 15 mins **Servings: 6**
Ingredients:
4 shallots, sliced
1/4 cup white wine
1/2 teaspoon chili powder
4 garlic cloves, chopped
6 pork chops
2 tablespoons canola oil
3 tablespoons maple syrup
Salt and pepper

Directions:
1. Heat the oil in a frying pan and add the pork chops. Fry on high heat for a few minutes until golden, then place in your slow cooker.
2. Add the remaining ingredients and season with salt and pepper.
3. Cover and cook on low for 4 hours.
4. Serve warm.

Autumn Pork Roast

Time: 6 hrs. 30 mins   **Servings: 6**
Ingredients:
2 cups butternut squash cubes
1 whole clove
Salt and pepper
2 thyme sprigs
1 bay leaf
1 star anise
1 pound pork shoulder, cubed
2 sweet potatoes, peeled and cubed
2 cups chicken stock
1 pound fresh pork sausages, sliced

Directions:
1. Place all ingredients in a crock pot.
2. Add salt and pepper to taste.
3. Cook on low for 6 hours.
4. Serve warm and fresh.

Onion Pork Chops with Creamy Mustard Sauce

Time: 5 hrs. 15 mins   **Servings: 4**
Ingredients
1 teaspoon dried mustard
1/4 teaspoon cayenne pepper
1/2 cup heavy cream
Salt and pepper
1 tablespoon apple cider vinegar
4 pork chops, bone in
2 onions, finely chopped
4 garlic cloves, minced
1/2 cup white wine
2 tablespoons Dijon mustard

Directions:
1. Mix all ingredients in your slow cooker.
2. Add salt and pepper and cook on low for 5 hours.
3. Serve warm.

Szechuan Roasted Pork

Time: 8 hrs. 15 mins   **Servings: 8**
Ingredients:
1 teaspoon sesame oil
1 teaspoon hot sauce
1 cup chicken stock
1 teaspoon garlic powder
1 cup water chestnuts, chopped
2 shallots, sliced
4 pounds pork shoulder, trimmed
1 can (8 oz.) bamboo shoots
1 tablespoon rice vinegar
2 tablespoons red bean paste
1 tablespoon Worcestershire sauce
1/4 cup soy sauce

Directions:
1. Mix all ingredients in your crock pot.
2. Cover and cook on low for 8 hours.
3. Serve warm.

Cola BBQ Pork Roast

Time: 8 hrs. 15 mins   **Servings: 6**
Ingredients:
2 onions, sliced
Salt and pepper
1 thyme sprig
1 red chili, chopped
1 cup BBQ sauce
1 cup cola
1 rosemary sprig
2 1/2 pounds pork shoulder, trimmed

Directions:
1. Mix all the ingredients in your crock pot.
2. Add salt and pepper
3. Cook the pork on low for 8 hours.
4. Serve warm.

Filipino Adobo Pork

Time: 7 hrs. 15 mins   **Servings: 8**
Ingredients:
1/4 cup soy sauce
1 cup water
6 garlic cloves, chopped
1/2 teaspoon chili powder
4 pounds pork roast
1/4 cup red wine vinegar
2 bay leaves
1 chipotle pepper, chopped

Directions:
1. Mix the vinegar, soy sauce, water, bay leaves, chipotle pepper, garlic and chili powder in a slow cooker.
2. Add the meat to the sauce and cover.
3. Cook on low for 7 hours.
4. Serve warm.

Sticky Glazed Pork Ribs

Time: 8 hrs. 15 mins   **Servings: 8**
Ingredients:
1/4 cup hoisin sauce
1 teaspoon garlic powder
2 shallots, chopped
2 tablespoons maple syrup
1 teaspoon onion powder
1 teaspoon grated ginger
2 tablespoons soy sauce
6 pounds short pork ribs
1 cup crushed pineapple in juice
1/2 cup spicy ketchup

Directions:
1. Mix all the ingredients in your slow cooker.
2. Stir until the ribs are evenly coated, then cover and cook on low for 8 hours.
3. Serve it warm.

Garlic Roasted Pork Belly

Time: 8 hrs. 15 mins   **Servings: 8**
Ingredients:
Salt and pepper
1 cup dry white wine
1 teaspoon cumin powder
1 teaspoon garlic powder
4 pounds pork belly
8 garlic cloves
1 teaspoon cayenne pepper

Directions:
1. Make a few holes in the pork meat and fill them with garlic cloves.
2. Sprinkle the meat with cumin, garlic powder, cayenne pepper, salt and pepper.
3. Place the pork belly in your slow cooker and add the wine.
4. Cook on low for 8 hours.
5. Serve warm.

Kahlua Pulled Pork

Time: 8 hrs. 15 mins   **Servings: 6**
Ingredients:
Salt and pepper
2 pounds pork shoulder
1/4 cup Kahlua liqueur
1 chipotle peppers, chopped
1/4 cup brewed coffee
1/2 cup chicken stock
2 bay leaves
1/2 teaspoon cumin seeds

Directions:
1. Combine all the ingredients in your slow cooker.
2. Add salt and pepper and cover.
3. Cook on low for 8 hours.
4. Serve it warm, shredded finely, either alone or in sandwiches.

Jerk Seasoning Pork Roast

Time: 6 hrs. 15 mins   **Servings: 6**
Ingredients:
1 teaspoon dried thyme
1 teaspoon dried mint
2 pounds pork roast
2 tablespoons Jamaican jerk seasoning
1 cup BBQ sauce
1/2 cup water
1 large onion, sliced
4 garlic cloves, chopped
Salt and pepper

Directions:
1. Sprinkle the pork with salt, pepper, mint, jerk seasoning and thyme.
2. Mix the onion, garlic, BBQ sauce and water in a slow cooker.
3. Place the pork over the sauce and cover.
4. Cook on low for 6 hours.
5. Serve warm.

Fruity Pork Tenderloin

Time: 8 hrs. 15 mins   **Servings: 8**
Ingredients:
1 star anise
Salt and pepper
1 cup apple juice
1 onion, chopped
1/2 cup chopped dried apricots
1/2 cup frozen cranberries
3 pounds pork tenderloin
1/2 pound plums, pitted and sliced
1/2 cup golden raisins
1/2 teaspoon garlic powder
1 cinnamon stick

Directions:
1. Mix the fruit, onion, garlic powder, spices, salt and pepper in your crock pot.
2. Place the pork tenderloin on top and cover.
3. Cook on low for 8 hours.
4. Serve warm, topped with the fruit.

Caribbean Sticky Pork Ribs

Time: 7 hrs. 15 mins   **Servings: 8**
Ingredients:
2 tablespoons honey
2 garlic cloves, chopped
Salt and pepper
1 teaspoon hot sauce
6 pounds pork ribs
1 can crushed pineapple
1/4 teaspoon chili powder
2 onions, sliced
1 teaspoon Worcestershire sauce
1/2 teaspoon all spice powder

Directions:
1. Mix the pineapple, honey, hot sauce, Worcestershire sauce, all spice and chili powder, salt and pepper, as well as onions and garlic in your slow cooker.
2. Place the pork ribs on top and drizzle with sauce.
3. Cover and cook on low for 7 hours.
4. Serve warm.

Pizza Pork Chops

Time: 6 hrs. 30 mins   **Servings: 6**
Ingredients:
6 pork chops
2 cups shredded mozzarella cheese
Salt and pepper
1 teaspoon dried oregano
1/2 cup pitted black olives, sliced
2 red bell peppers, cored and sliced
1 1/2 cups tomato sauce

Directions:
1. Put the pork chops in your slow cooker.
2. Add tomato sauce, oregano, black olives, salt and pepper.
3. Cover with a layer of shredded mozzarella cheese.
4. Cook on low for 6 hours.
5. Serve warm.

Apple Cherry Pork Chops

Time: 3 hrs. 15 mins   **Servings: 6**
Ingredients:
1 cup frozen sour cherries
1 onion, chopped
1 bay leaf
Salt and pepper
1 garlic clove, minced
1/2 cup apple cider vinegar
6 pork chops
4 red, tart apples, cored and sliced
1/2 cup tomato sauce

Directions:
1. Mix all ingredients in your slow cooker.
2. Add salt and pepper and cook on high for 3 hours.
3. Serve warm and fresh.

Mango Chutney Pork Chops

Time: 5 hrs. 15 mins   **Servings: 4**
Ingredients:
Salt and pepper
3/4 cup chicken stock
1 bay leaf
4 pork chops
1 jar mango chutney

Directions:
1. Mix all the ingredients in your crock pot.
2. Add salt and pepper to taste and cook on low for 5 hours.
3. Serve warm.

Smoky Apple Butter Pork Chops

Time: 4 hrs. 30 mins   **Servings: 4**
Ingredients:
4 pork chops
1 bay leaf
Salt and pepper
1 teaspoon smoked paprika
6 bacon slices, chopped
1 tablespoon butter
1 cup apple butter
1/2 cup tomato sauce

Directions:
1. Place a frying pan over medium heat and add the bacon. Cook until crisp, then add the butter and pork chops.
2. Fry for 2 minutes until golden, then place in your slow cooker.
3. Add the remaining ingredients and season with salt and pepper.
4. Cook on low for 4 hours. Serve warm.

Roasted Rosemary Pork and Potatoes

Time: 6 hrs. 30 mins   **Servings: 6**
Ingredients:
2 rosemary sprigs
Salt and pepper
1 1/2 pounds potatoes, peeled and cubed
2 pounds pork roast, cubed
3 large carrots, sliced
1 cup chicken stock
1 celery root, peeled and cubed

Directions:
1. Mix the pork roast, carrots, celery, potatoes, rosemary and stock in your crock pot.
2. Add salt and pepper and cook on low for 6 hours.
3. Serve warm.

Three-Pepper Roasted Pork Tenderloin

Time: 8 hrs. 15 mins   **Servings: 8**

Ingredients:
1/4 cup three pepper mix
Salt and pepper
3 pounds pork tenderloin
2 tablespoons Dijon mustard
1 cup chicken stock

Directions:

1. Mix the pork tenderloin with salt and pepper.
2. Spread the meat with mustard. Spread the pepper mix on your chopping board then roll the pork through this mixture.
3. Place in your crock pot and add the stock.
4. Cook on low for 8 hours.
5. Serve it warm with your favorite side dish.

Intense Mustard Pork Chops

Time: 5 hrs. 15 mins   **Servings: 4**

Ingredients:
Salt and pepper
1 tablespoon honey
1 shallot, finely chopped
4 garlic cloves, minced
2 tablespoons olive oil
4 pork chops
2 tablespoons Dijon mustard
1 cup chicken stock

Directions:

1. Rub the pork chops with salt and pepper and place them in your crock pot.
2. Add the remaining ingredients and additional salt and pepper to taste.
3. Cover and cook on low for 5 hours.
4. Serve the pork chops topped with sauce.

Cuban-Style Pork Roast Over Simple Black Beans

Time: 6 hrs. 15 mins   **Servings: 6**

Ingredients:
1/2 cup chicken stock
4 garlic cloves, minced
1/2 teaspoon cumin powder
1 lime, juiced
1 large onion, sliced
1/2 teaspoon chili powder
1 teaspoon smoked paprika
Salt and pepper
2 pounds pork roast, trimmed and cubed
1/2 cup fresh orange juice
Canned black beans for serving

Directions:

1. Mix the pork roast with the remaining ingredients in your slow cooker.
2. Add salt and pepper and cook on low for 6 hours.
3. Serve the pork roast over canned black beans.

Honey Apple Pork Chops

Time: 5 hrs. 15 mins   **Servings: 4**

Ingredients:
2 tablespoons honey
Salt and pepper
1 shallot, chopped
1 red chili, chopped
1 heirloom tomato, peeled and diced
2 garlic cloves, chopped
4 pork chops
2 red, tart apples, peeled, cored and cubed
1 tablespoon olive oil
1 cup apple cider

Directions:

1. Mix all the ingredients in your crock pot.
2. Add salt and pepper to taste.
3. Cook on low for 5 hours.
4. Serve warm.

CHAPTER 8

BEEF RECIPES

Caramelized Onion Pot Roast

Time: 8 hrs. 30 mins   **Servings: 8**
Ingredients:
4 garlic cloves, chopped
1/2 cup water
Salt and pepper to taste
2 carrots, sliced
1 celery root, peeled and cubed
4 pounds beef roast
4 large onions, sliced
3 tablespoons canola oil
2 large potatoes, peeled and cubed
1 cup beef stock

Directions:
1. Add the onions to the oil as it is heating in a frying pan.
2. Cook for 10 mins, or until golden brown and just beginning to caramelize.
3. Add the remaining ingredients to your slow cooker after transferring.
4. Cook on low for 8 hours after seasoning with adequate salt and pepper.
5. Serve the pot roast hot.

Layered Enchilada Casserole

Time: 6 hrs. 15 mins   **Servings: 6**
Ingredients:
1 pound ground beef
2 tablespoons canola oil
1 leek, sliced
1 shallot, chopped
4 garlic cloves, chopped
2 cups sliced mushrooms
2 cups enchilada sauce
6 flour tortillas, shredded
2 cups grated Cheddar
Salt and pepper to taste

Directions:
1. Heat the oil in a skillet and add the beef. Cook for some minutes, stirring often then add the shallot, leek, and garlic and remove from heat.
2. Place the enchilada sauce, cooked beef, mushrooms, and tortillas in your slow cooker.
3. Top with cheese and cook on low for 6 hours.
4. Serve the casserole warm.

French Onion Sandwich Filling

Time: 9 hrs. 15 mins   **Servings: 10**
Ingredients:
4 pounds beef roast
4 sweet onions, sliced
4 bacon slices, chopped
1 teaspoon garlic powder
1/2 cup white wine
Salt and pepper to taste
1 thyme sprig

Directions:
1. In your crock pot, combine all the ingredients.
2. Season with salt and pepper and cook for 9 hours on low.
3. Once the meat is done, shred it into threads and use it as a sandwich filling, either hot or cold.

Beef Roast with Shallots and Potatoes

Time: 7 hrs. 30 mins   **Servings: 6**
Ingredients:
1 1/2 pounds beef chuck
2 large onions, sliced
6 shallots, peeled
1 1/2 pounds potatoes, peeled and halved
1 cup beef stock
1/2 cup white wine
1 thyme sprig
1 rosemary sprig
Salt and pepper to taste

Directions:
1. In your crock pot, combine all the ingredients.
2. Season with salt and pepper and cook for 7 hours on low.
3. Serve warm.

Beef Roast with Shiitake Mushrooms

Time: 7 hrs. 15 mins   **Servings: 8**
Ingredients:
1/2 pound baby carrots
1 thyme sprig
Salt and pepper to taste
1/4 cup low sodium soy sauce
1 tablespoon rice vinegar
1 1/2 cups beef stock
3 pounds beef roast
1/2 pound shiitake mushrooms

Directions:
1. In your crock pot, combine all the ingredients.
2. After adding salt and pepper, cook on low for 7 hours.
3. Serve the mushrooms either hot or cold.

Tangy Italian Shredded Beef

Time: 8 hrs. 15 mins   **Servings: 8**
Ingredients:
1/4 cup white wine
1 tablespoon honey
1 teaspoon Italian seasoning
4 pounds beef sirloin roast, trimmed of fat
1 lemon, juiced
Salt and pepper to taste
1/2 cup tomato juice
1 rosemary sprig

Directions:
1. Combine all the ingredients in your crock cooker.
2. Cook on low for 8 hours.
3. Serve alone or put in sandwiches or wraps.

Southern Beef Pot Roast

Time: 8 hrs. 15 mins   **Servings: 8**
Ingredients:
1/2 pound baby carrots
1 cup red salsa
1 cup beef stock
3 pounds beef sirloin roast
8 medium size potatoes, peeled and halved
Salt and pepper to taste
1 thyme sprig

Directions:
1. Combine all ingredients in the slow cooker.
2. Season with salt and pepper, then cook on low for 8 hours.
3. Serve warm.

Beef Zucchini Stew

Time: 2 hrs. 45 mins   **Servings: 6**
Ingredients:
1/4 teaspoon cumin seeds
Salt and pepper to taste
1 can fire-roasted tomatoes
1/2 cup beef stock
2 bay leaves
1/4 teaspoon paprika
1 pound ground beef
2 tablespoons canola oil
1 leek, sliced
2 garlic cloves, minced
3 zucchinis, sliced

Directions:
1. Add the beef to the hot oil in a frying pan. Stirring frequently, cook for a few minutes, then place in the crock pot.
2. Fill the slow cooker with the remaining ingredients.
3. Add salt and pepper, then cook on high for 2 1/2 hours.
4. Serve warm.

Sloppy Joes

Time: 7 hrs. 15 mins   **Servings: 8**
Ingredients:
Buns for serving
1/4 cup spicy ketchup
1/2 cup tomato juice
1/2 cup beef stock
2 pounds ground beef
2 large onions, finely chopped
1 tablespoon Worcestershire sauce
Salt and pepper to taste

Directions:
1. Fill your slow cooker with all the ingredients.
2. Season with salt and pepper and cook for 7 hours on low.
3. Serve on buns.

Cowboy Beef

Time: 6 hrs. 15 mins   **Servings: 6**
Ingredients:
4 garlic cloves, chopped
Salt and pepper to taste
Coleslaw for serving
1 can (15 oz.) red beans, drained
1 cup BBQ sauce
2 1/2 pounds beef sirloin roast
6 bacon slices, chopped
2 onions, sliced
1 teaspoon chili powder

Directions:
1. Combine the beef sirloin, bacon, onions, and garlic. Add the red beans, BBQ sauce, chili powder, salt, and pepper.
2. Cook for six hours on low.
3. Top the beef with fresh coleslaw and serve hot.

Vegetable Beef Roast with Horseradish

Time: 6 hrs. 30 mins   **Servings: 8**
Ingredients:
1 celery root, peeled and cubed
1 cup beef stock
1 cup water
Salt and pepper to taste
2 onions, quartered
2 cups sliced mushrooms
2 cups snap peas
4 pounds beef roast, trimmed of fat
4 large potatoes, peeled and halved
2 large carrots, sliced
1/4 cup prepared horseradish for serving

Directions:
1. Combine everything in your crock pot and season with salt & pepper.
2. Cook for six hours on low.
3. Serve hot with horseradish on the side.

Sweet and Tangy Short Ribs

Time: 9 hrs. 15 mins   **Servings: 8**
Ingredients:
1/4 cup balsamic vinegar
1 teaspoon garlic powder
1 teaspoon cumin powder
Salt and pepper to taste
1/4 cup brown sugar
2 tablespoons hot sauce
6 pounds short ribs
2 cups BBQ sauce
2 red onions, sliced
2 tablespoons apricot preserves
2 tablespoons Worcestershire sauce
1 tablespoon Dijon mustard

Directions:
1. In your crock pot, combine the BBQ sauce, onions, vinegar, sugar, preserved apricots, Worcestershire sauce, mustard, garlic powder, and cumin powder.
2. Add the short ribs and thoroughly coat.
3. Cook for 9 hours on low.
4. Serve hot.

Bavarian Beef Roast

Time: 10 hrs. 15 mins **Servings: 6**
Ingredients:
1/2 cup beef stock
Salt and pepper to taste
2 tablespoons mustard seeds
1 teaspoon prepared horseradish
2 pounds beef roast
2 tablespoons all-purpose flour
1 cup apple juice

Directions:
1. Add flour and season the beef with salt and pepper.
2. Fill your crock pot with the beef roast and the remaining ingredients.
3. Season with salt and pepper as necessary, then cook on low for 10 hours.
4. Serve warm.

Beef Stroganoff

Time: 6 hrs. 15 mins **Servings: 6**
Ingredients:
Cooked pasta for serving
1 tablespoon Worcestershire sauce
1/2 cup water
1 cup cream cheese
Salt and pepper to taste
1 1/2 pounds beef stew meat, cubed
1 large onion, chopped
4 garlic cloves, minced

Directions:
1. Combine all the ingredients in a crock pot.
2. Add salt and pepper, then cook on low for six hours.
3. Combine the cooked pasta of your choice with the heated stroganoff.

Pepperoncini Beef Stew

Time: 7 hrs. 15 mins **Servings: 8**
Ingredients:
1 bay leaf
Salt and pepper to taste
1 large onion, finely chopped
1 celery stalk, diced
4 red bell peppers, cored and sliced
2 pounds beef roast, cubed
2 tablespoons canola oil
6 garlic cloves, minced
1 jar pepperoncini
1 can fire roasted tomatoes

Directions:
1. Add the roast to a frying pan with the canola oil already hot.
2. Cook until golden brown on all sides, then transfer to your crock pot.
3. Fill your crock pot with the remaining ingredients.
3. Season with salt and pepper and cook for 7 hours on low.
4. Serve hot.

Corned Beef with Sauerkraut

Time: 8 hrs. 15 mins **Servings: 6**
Ingredients:
1 cup beef stock
Salt and pepper to taste
1 pound sauerkraut, shredded
1 onion, sliced
1/2 teaspoon cumin seeds
3 pounds corned beef brisket
4 large carrots, sliced

Directions:
1. In your crock pot, combine all the ingredients.
2. Add salt and pepper, then cook on low for 8 hours.
3. When done thinly slice the beef and serve with the sauerkraut.

Mexican Braised Beef

Time: 8 hrs. 15 mins   **Servings: 8**
Ingredients:
1 cup beef stock
Salt and pepper to taste
4 pounds beef roast
1/2 teaspoon cumin powder
1 can fire roasted tomatoes
1 cup frozen corn
1/2 teaspoon garlic powder
2 chipotle peppers, chopped
1 teaspoon chili powder
1/2 teaspoon cayenne pepper

Directions:
1. In your crock pot, combine the peppers, stock, tomatoes, frozen corn, garlic powder, chili powder, cayenne pepper, and cumin powder.
2. Add salt and pepper, then cook on low for 8 hours.
3. Serve warm.

Bell Pepper Steak

Time: 6 hrs. 15 mins   **Servings: 4**
Ingredients:
1 tablespoon soy sauce
Salt and pepper to taste
2 red bell peppers, cored and sliced
2 yellow bell peppers, cored and sliced
1 tablespoon brown sugar
2 pounds beef sirloin, cut into thin strips
4 garlic cloves, chopped
2 shallots, sliced
1 tablespoon apple cider vinegar

Directions:
1. In your slow cooker, combine the beef sirloin, garlic, shallots, bell peppers, sugar, vinegar, soy sauce, salt, and pepper.
2. Cover and cook on low for 6 hours.
3. Serve warm.

Tomato Beef Stew

Time: 5 hrs. 15 mins   **Servings: 6**
Ingredients:
4 garlic cloves, minced
1/2 teaspoon dried oregano
Salt and pepper to taste
4 heirloom tomatoes, peeled and cubed
1 cup beef stock
2 pounds beef roast, cubed
2 tablespoons canola oil
1 shallot, sliced
1/2 teaspoon cumin powder

Directions:
1. Add the steak to the hot oil in a frying pan. After cooking for 5 minutes or until golden, place in crock pot.
2. Add the other ingredients and sprinkle salt and pepper over everything.
3. Cook on low for five hours, then serve.

Beef Roast au Jus

Time: 10 hrs. 15 mins   **Servings: 8**
Ingredients:
4 pounds rump roast
1 teaspoon chili powder
1 teaspoon garlic powder
1 tablespoon ground black pepper
1 cup water
Salt and pepper to taste
1 tablespoon smoked paprika
1 teaspoon mustard seeds

Directions:
1. In a bowl, combine the salt, pepper, black pepper, paprika, chili powder, garlic powder, and mustard seeds.
2. Apply this mixture to the beef and thoroughly rub it into the flesh.
3. Add the water to the crock pot with the beef.
4. Cover and cook for 10 hours on low.

Coffee Beef Roast

Time: 4 hrs. 15 mins   Servings: 6
Ingredients:
4 garlic cloves, minced
Salt and pepper to taste
1 cup strong brewed coffee
2 pounds beef sirloin
2 tablespoons olive oil
1/2 cup beef stock

Directions:
1. Combine all the ingredients in your slow cooker and season with salt & pepper.
2. Cover and cook for 4 hours on high.
3. Serve hot.

Root Vegetable Beef Stew

Time: 8 hrs. 30 mins   Servings: 8
Ingredients:
1 celery root, peeled and cubed
1 lemon, juiced
1 teaspoon Worcestershire sauce
1 cup beef stock
Salt and pepper to taste
4 garlic cloves, chopped
4 large potatoes, peeled and cubed
3 pounds beef sirloin roast, cubed
4 carrots, sliced
2 parsnips, sliced
1 turnip, peeled and cubed
1 bay leaf

Directions:
1. In your crock pot, combine the beef, stock, bay leaf, lemon juice, carrots, parsnips, celery root, garlic, potatoes, and turnips.
2. Add salt and pepper before covering
3. Cook for 8 hours on low.
4. Serve warm.

Hamburger Beef Casserole

Time: 7 hrs. 30 mins   Servings: 6
Ingredients:
1 cup processed meat, shredded
1 cup grated Cheddar cheese
1 celery stalk, sliced
2 onions, sliced
1 cup green peas
1 1/2 pounds beef sirloin, cut into thin trips
2 large potatoes, peeled and finely sliced
1 can condensed cream of mushroom soup
Salt and pepper to taste

Directions:
1. In your crock pot, combine the beef, potatoes, celery stalk, green peas, mushroom soup, salt, and pepper.
2. Add both cheeses on top, then cover.
3. Cook on low for 7 hours.
4. Serve warm.

Texas-Style Braised Beef

Servings: 8
Time: 8 hrs. 15 mins
Ingredients:
2 green chili peppers, chopped
1/2 teaspoon garlic powder
1/2 teaspoon chili powder
Salt and pepper to taste
1 shallot, chopped
4 pounds beef sirloin roast
2 chipotle peppers, chopped
1 cup BBQ sauce
2 tablespoons brown sugar

Directions
1. In the crockpot, combine the chipotle peppers, green chili peppers, shallot, BBQ sauce, brown sugar, garlic powder, chili powder, and salt and pepper to taste.
2. Add the beef and thoroughly coat it with this mixture.
3. Cook on low settings for 8 hours while covered.
4. Slice the steak and serve it hot.

Carne Guisada

Time: 6 hrs. 30 mins   **Servings: 8**
Ingredients:
3 garlic cloves, minced
1 1/2 cups beef stock
1 cup tomato sauce
Salt and pepper to taste
4 medium size potatoes, peeled and cubed
1/4 teaspoon chili powder
1/2 teaspoon cumin powder
3 pounds beef chuck roast, cut into small cubes
2 red bell peppers, cored and diced
2 shallots, chopped

Directions:
1. Put the chuck roast in your crock pot with the bell peppers, shallots, garlic, tomatoes, chili powder, cumin powder, stock, and tomato sauce.
2. Add salt and pepper as desired, then cook on low for 6 hours.
3. Serve with burritos or tortillas.

Red Wine Onion Braised Beef

Time: 7 hrs. 15 mins   **Servings: 8**
Ingredients:
1 teaspoon cumin powder
Salt and pepper to taste
2 red onions, sliced
1 thyme sprig
2 pounds beef chuck roast
1 cup red wine
1 teaspoon ground coriander

Directions:
1. Use salt, pepper, coriander, and cumin powder to season the beef roast.
2. Add the remaining ingredients to your crock pot with the meat.
3. Cook on low for 7 hours.
4. Serve warm.

Beer-Braised Beef

Time: 8 hrs. 15 mins   **Servings: 6**
Ingredients:
1/4 cup beef stock
Salt and pepper to taste
2 large potatoes, peeled and cubed
4 garlic cloves, chopped
1 thyme sprig
1 cup dark beer
1 celery stalk, sliced
2 pounds beef sirloin
1/2 pound baby carrots
1 large sweet onion, chopped

Directions:
1. Combine all the ingredients in your crock pot and season with salt & pepper.
2. Cover and cook on low for 8 hours.
3. Serve warm.

Marinara Flank Steaks

Time: 5 hrs. 15 mins   **Servings: 4**
Ingredients:
1 cup shredded mozzarella cheese
1 tablespoon balsamic vinegar
1 teaspoon Italian seasoning
4 flank steaks
2 cups marinara sauce
Salt and pepper to taste

Directions:
1. Put the steaks in the slow cooker.
2. Add the cheese on top after thoroughly mixing the marinara sauce, balsamic vinegar, Italian seasoning, salt, and pepper.
3. Cover and cook on low for 5 hours.
4. While the cheese is still gooey, serve the steaks and sauce warm.

Ground Beef BBQ

Time: 7 hrs. 15 mins   **Servings: 8**
Ingredients:
1 1/2 cups BBQ sauce
1/2 cup beef broth
Salt and pepper to taste
4 garlic cloves, chopped
2 celery stalks, chopped
3 pounds ground beef
1 large onion, chopped
1 tablespoon apple cider vinegar
1 teaspoon Dijon mustard
1 tablespoon brown sugar

Directions:
1. In your crock pot, combine all the ingredients.
2. Cook on low for 7 hours after adding salt and pepper.
3. Serve hot.

Beef Okra Tomato Stew

Time: 6 hrs. 15 mins   **Servings: 6**
Ingredients:
Salt and pepper to taste
Chopped parsley for serving
1 can (15 oz.) diced tomatoes
12 oz. frozen okra, chopped
2 large potatoes, peeled and cubed
1 cup beef stock
1 1/2 pounds beef roast, cut into thin strips
1 large onion, chopped
4 garlic cloves, minced
1 thyme sprig

Directions:
1. Fill the crock pot with the beef roast, onion, garlic, tomatoes, okra, potatoes, stock, and thyme sprig.
2. Add salt and pepper, then cook on low for six hours.
3. Top the stew with chopped parsley and serve hot or cold.

Beef Barbacoa

Time: 6 hrs. 30 mins   **Servings: 8**
Ingredients:
6 garlic cloves, chopped
1 1/2 teaspoons chili powder
Salt and pepper to taste
3 tablespoons white wine vinegar
4 pounds beef chuck roast
2 red onions, sliced
1 1/2 cups tomato sauce

Directions:
1. Combine everything in your crock pot.
2. Cook on low for 6 hours.
3. Serve warm.

Caribe Pot Roast

Time: 8 hrs. 15 mins   **Servings: 8**
Ingredients:
1 celery stalk, sliced
1/2 teaspoon dried oregano
Salt and pepper to taste
2 tablespoons brown sugar
1 1/2 cups tomato sauce
4 pounds boneless beef chuck roast
4 garlic cloves, chopped
2 large onions, sliced
1 tablespoon cocoa powder
1 teaspoon chili powder
1/2 teaspoon cumin powder

Directions:
1. Combine all ingredients in the slow cooker.
2. Add salt and pepper, then cook for 8 hours on low.
3. Serve hot or cold.

Apple Corned Beef with Red Cabbage

Time: 6 hrs. 30 mins   **Servings: 6**
Ingredients:
2 red apples, cored and diced
1 bay leaf
Salt and pepper to taste
1 cinnamon stick
1 star anise
1/2 cup red wine
1 1/2 pounds beef chuck roast, cubed
1 red cabbage, shredded
1/2 teaspoon cumin seeds
1 tablespoon red wine vinegar
1/2 cup beef stock

Directions:
1. In your crock pot, combine the apples, cabbage, cumin seeds, cinnamon, star anise, red wine, and vinegar.
2. Add the salt, pepper, and bay leaf, and cook on low for 6 hours.
3. Serve warm.

Chunky Beef Pasta Sauce

Time: 6 hrs. 30 mins   **Servings: 8**
Ingredients:
1 cup tomato sauce
1 bay leaf
Salt and pepper to taste
2 garlic cloves, chopped
1 can (28 oz.) diced tomatoes
2 pounds beef sirloin, cut into thin strips
1 carrot, diced
1 celery stalk, diced
2 cups sliced mushrooms
1/4 cup red wine

Directions:
1. In your slow cooker, combine all ingredients.
2. Cover and cook for 6 hours on low.
3. Serve immediately.

Hot Corned Beef

Time: 6 hrs. 15 mins   **Servings: 6**
Ingredients:
Salt and pepper to taste
2 tablespoons balsamic vinegar
1 tablespoon Dijon mustard
2 pounds corned beef
1 cup beef stock
2 chipotle peppers, chopped

Directions:
1. In your crock pot, combine the stock, vinegar, mustard, and chipotle peppers.
2. Add the corned beef.
3. If necessary, season with salt and pepper and cook on low for 6 hours.
4. Serve warm.

Mediterranean Beef Brisket

Time: 7 hrs. 30 mins   **Servings: 8**
Ingredients:
1/2 cup dry red wine
1 thyme sprig
Salt and pepper to taste
1/2 cup pitted Kalamata olives, sliced
4 pounds beef brisket
1 can (15 oz.) diced tomatoes
4 garlic cloves, chopped
1 rosemary sprig

Directions:
1. In your crock pot, combine the tomatoes, red wine, Kalamata olives, garlic, thyme, and rosemary.
2. Add salt and pepper, then cover.
3. Cook on low for 7 hours.
4. Serve hot or cold, topped with sauce.

Sriracha-Style Corned Beef

Time: 5 hrs. 15 mins   **Servings: 6**
Ingredients:
1/2 cup beef stock
Salt and pepper to taste
4 garlic cloves, chopped
1/2 teaspoon onion powder
1 tablespoon Sriracha
2 pounds corned beef
1/4 cup low-sodium soy sauce
2 tablespoons brown sugar
1 teaspoon sesame oil
1 tablespoon rice vinegar
2 shallots, sliced

Directions:
1. In your crock pot, combine the Sriracha, sesame oil, vinegar, shallots, soy sauce, sugar, garlic, stock, and onion powder.
2. Add the beef and thoroughly cover with sauce.
3. If necessary, add salt and pepper, then cook on low for 5 hours. Serve.

Curried Beef Short Ribs

Time: 8 hrs. 15 mins   **Servings: 6**
Ingredients:
1 lime, juiced
Salt and pepper to taste
1 cup tomato sauce
1 teaspoon curry powder
1/2 teaspoon garlic powder
4 pounds beef short ribs
3 tablespoons red curry paste
2 shallots, chopped
1 teaspoon grated ginger

Directions:
1. In a crock pot, combine the tomato sauce, curry paste, curry powder, garlic powder, shallots, ginger, and lime juice.
2. After adding salt and pepper, add the ribs to the pot.
3. Thoroughly coat the ribs with sauce.
4. Cover and cook on low for 8 hours.
5. Serve warm.

Gruyere Flank Steaks

Time: 3 hrs. 15 mins   **Servings: 4**
Ingredients:
4 flank steaks
1/2 cup cream cheese
1 teaspoon Dijon mustard
Salt and pepper to taste
Salt and pepper to taste
1 cup crumbled gruyere cheese
1/2 cup white wine
1 teaspoon Worcestershire sauce

Directions:
1. Sprinkle salt and pepper on the steaks, then put them in your slow cooker.
2. In a bowl, combine the other ingredients; then, spread the mixture over the steaks.
3. Cook the food for three hours on high with the lid on.
4. Serve your favorite side dish and the steaks warm.

Collard Green Beef Sauté

Time: 3 hrs. 15 mins   **Servings: 6**
Ingredients:
1/4 cup beef stock
Salt and pepper to taste
1/2 teaspoon cumin powder
2 tablespoons canola oil
2 bunches collard greens, shredded
1 1/2 pounds beef roast, cut into thin strips
1 tablespoon all-purpose flour

Directions:
1. Rub the beef with salt and pepper, then again with flour and cumin powder.
2. Heat the oil in a skillet and cook the beef for a few minutes on each side, then place in the crock pot.
3. Add the remaining ingredients and cover.
4. Cook for 3 hours on the highest setting.
5. Serve hot and fresh.

CONCLUSION

A crockpot is just what the name suggests: a slow cooker. This appliance simmers and ferments the food, making it a popular item used worldwide for different purposes. Crockpots are traditionally made of ceramic, but there are also some made from plastic or steel. Crockpots are available in various sizes, shapes, and colors. Their versatility is limitless, depending on the recipes or ingredients you are using. Aside from being used as a slow-cookers, crockpots can also be used to heat water and even as an alternative to ovens.

Preparation of food in a crockpot is easy because most of it can be prepared and kept warm until you are ready to consume it. This saves you time from having to slave over a hot stove for hours just to prepare your meals ahead of time.

The crockpot is also perfect for small families because you can always perform other tasks during the preparation of the meal. You don't have to be in the kitchen for hours, just waiting and hoping that your crockpot warms up or that it will cook your food once it's filled up.

Rather than having to spend upwards of $100 on a full-sized, large-capacity stove-top cooker with a lot of dishes and cooking utensils you will never use again, you can purchase a cheap crockpot for as little as $20 and use less space in your cabinets. You will be able to enjoy what you are preparing and not worry about how it's going to taste.

Vital information about crockpots and delicious recipes have been provided in each chapter of this book. It's time for you to prepare tasty foods with your new crockpot!

INDEX

Buttered Hot Rum	101
Butternut Squash Creamy Soup	51
Buttery Chocolate Cake	79
Button Mushroom Chicken Stew	47

C

Caramel Cider	100
Caramel Hot Chocolate	98
Caramel Pear Pudding Cake	71
Caramelized Onion Pot Roast	125
Caramelized Onion Dip	21
Caramelized Onion Chicken Stew	48
Cardamom Coconut Rice Pudding	76
Caribbean Sticky Pork Ribs	121
Caribe Pot Roast	132
Carne Guisada	131
Cheddar Pork Casserole	118
Cheddar Rice	85
Cheeseburger Dip	24
Cheesy Bacon Dip	22
Cheesy Beef Dip	31
Cheesy Chicken	43
Cheesy Chicken Bites	23
Cheesy Mushroom Dip	28
Cherry Cider	96
Chicken Barley Squash Salad	36
Chicken Black Olive Stew	41
Chicken Cacciatore	49
Chicken Cauliflower Gratin	42
Chicken Cordon Bleu	45
Chicken Enchilada Soup	57
Chicken Layered Potato Casserole	38
Chicken Ravioli in Tomato Sauce	46
Chicken Rice Soup	58
Chicken Sausage Soup	56
Chicken Stroganoff	44
Chicken Sweet Potato Stew	37
Chicken Taco Filling	37
Chicken Tikka Masala	43
Chili BBQ Ribs	107
Chili Boston Baked Beans	82

Chili Chicken Wings	23
Chili Verde	104
Chipotle BBQ Meatballs	23
Chipotle BBQ Sausage Bites	23
Chocolate Hot Coffee	96
Chocolate Walnut Bread	73
Chunky Beef Pasta Sauce	133
Chunky Mushroom Soup	63
Chunky Potato Ham Soup	61
Chunky Pumpkin and Kale Soup	63
Cider Braised Chicken	41
Citrus Bourbon Cocktail	93
Citrus Green Tea	95
Coconut Condensed Milk Custard	79
Coconut Poached Pears	72
Coconut Squash Soup	54
Coffee Beef Roast	130
Cola BBQ Pork Roast	119
Collard Green Beef Sauté	134
Corn and Red Pepper Chowder	63
Corned Beef with Sauerkraut	128
Country Style Pork Ribs	104
Cowboy Beef	127
Cranberry Sauce Meatballs	24
Cranberry Spiced Tea	89
Cranberry Stuffed Apples	68
Cream Cheese Chicken	37
Creamy Bacon Soup	51
Creamy Cauliflower Soup	60
Creamy Chicken and Mushroom Pot Pie	46
Creamy Chicken Stew	44
Creamy Coconut Tapioca Pudding	69
Creamy Dijon Pork Shoulder	110
Creamy Leek and Potato Soup	62
Creamy Noodle Soup	61
Creamy Potato Soup	54
Creamy Potatoes	34
Creamy Spinach Dip	22
Creamy Tortellini Soup	64

Hot Marmalade Cider	98
Hot Spicy Apple Cider	92
Hot Whiskey Sour	98
Hungarian Borscht	58

I

Intense Mustard Pork Chops	123
Irish Cream Coffee	101
Italian Wedding Soup	54
Italian Barley Soup	57
Italian Fennel Braised Chicken	47
Italian Style Pork Shoulder	105

J

Jerk Seasoning Pork Roast	121

K

Kahlua Coffee	96
Kahlua Pulled Pork	120
Kielbasa Kale Soup	60
Korean BBQ Chicken	42

L

Lavender Blackberry Crumble	67
Layered Enchilada Casserole	125
Leek Potato Soup	62
Lemon Berry Cake	71
Lemon Garlic Roasted Chicken	46
Lemon Lime Jasmine Tea	99
Lemon Roasted Pork Tenderloin	107
Lemon Vegetable Pork Roast	117
Lemonade Cider	93
Lemony Salmon Soup	61
Lima Bean Soup	57

M

Makes-A-Meal Baked Beans	85
Mango Chicken Sauté	45

Mango Chutney Pork Chops	122
Mango Flavored Pulled Pork	108
Maple Bourbon Mulled Cider	91
Maple Roasted Pears	77
Maple Syrup Glazed Carrots	30
Maraschino Cherry Cola Cake	74
Marinara Flank Steaks	131
Marsala Pork Chops	110
Mediterranean Beef Brisket	133
Mediterranean Dip	25
Medley Vegetable Chicken Stew	42
Mexican Beef Soup	58
Mexican Braised Beef	129
Mexican Chicken Stew	48
Mexican Chili Dip	28
Mexican Dip	19
Mexican Pork Roast	105
Minestrone Soup	62
Miso Braised Pork	112
Mixed Nut Brownies	78
Mixed Olive Dip	27
Molten Chocolate Cake Mulled	73
Cranberry Punch Mulled Pink	94
Wine	95
Mulled Wine	89
Multigrain Chicken Pilaf	36
Mushroom Pork Stew	118

N

Nacho Sauce	20
Navy Bean Stew	113
Never-Fail Rice	82
No Crust Lemon Cheesecake	74
No-Meat Baked Beans	85
Nutella Hot Chocolate	94
Nutty Pear Streusel	70

O

Oat-Topped Apples	69
Okra Vegetable Soup	58
One Bowl Chocolate Cake	69

Onion Pork Chops with Creamy Mustard Sauce 119
Onion Pork Tenderloin 104
Orange Brandy Hot Toddy 99
Orange Ginger Cheesecake 72
Orange Glazed Chicken 36
Orange Salmon Soup 64
Oriental Chicken Bites 29

P

Paprika Chicken Wings 38
Parmesan Chicken 40
Party Cranberry Punch 100
Party Mix 20
Peachy Cider 97
Peanut Butter Chocolate Chip Bars 78
Peanut Butter Pork Belly 116
Peppermint Chocolate Clusters 79
Peppermint Hot Chocolate 99
Pepperoncini Beef Stew 128
Pepperoni Pizza Dip 34
Pimiento Cheese Dip 32
Pineapple Baked Beans 87
Pineapple Coconut Tapioca Pudding 76
Pineapple Cranberry Pork Ham 105
Pineapple Upside Down Cake 67
Pinto Bean Chili Soup 51
Pizza Dip 26
Pizza Pork Chops 121
Pizza Rice 86
Pomegranate Cider 97
Pork and Corn Soup 65
Pork Belly over Smoky Sauerkraut 117
Pork Chickpea Stew 116
Pork & Ham Dip 24
Pork Sausage Stew 109
Portobello Mushroom Soup 65
Posole Soup 52
Potato Kielbasa Soup 59
Pretzel Party Mix 30

Provencal Beef Soup 52
Pulled Chicken 44
Pumpkin Croissant Pudding 70
Pure Berry Crumble 68

Q

Queso Verde Dip 20
Quick Layered Appetizer 29
Quick Lentil & Ham Soup 54

R

Raspberry Brownie Cake 67
Raspberry Hot Chocolate 94
Red Bean and Brown Rice Stew 84
Red Bean Pork Stew 112
Red Beans & Rice 115
Red Cabbage Pork Stew 117
Red Chili Pulled Pork 109
Red Chili Quinoa Soup 63
Red Salsa Chicken 48
Red Wine Braised Pork Ribs 103
Red Wine Chicken and Mushroom Stew 38
Red Wine Onion Braised Beef 131
Refried Beans with Bacon 85
Rice 'n Beans 'n Salsa 83
Rich Chocolate Peanut Butter Cake 69
Ricotta Lemon Cake 77
Risi Bisi (Peas and Rice) 83
Roasted Bell Pepper Pork Stew 109
Roasted Bell Pepper Quinoa Soup 62
Roasted Bell Peppers Dip 32
Roasted Rosemary Pork and Potatoes 122
Rocky Road Chocolate Cake 77
Root Vegetable Beef Stew 130
Rosemary Mulled Cider 89
Rosemary Potatoes 21

S

S'Mores Fondue	79
Salted Caramel Milk Steamer	90
Saucy Apples and Pears	80
Sauerkraut Cumin Pork	106
Sausage and Pepper Appetizer	33
Sausage Bean Soup	53
Sausage Dip	18
Sesame Glazed Chicken Silky	43
Chocolate Fondue	72
Sloppy Joes	127
Slow-Cooked Pork in Tomato Sauce	111
Smoked Ham and Lima Bean Stew	112
Smoky Apple Butter Pork Chops	122
Smoky Beans	87
Smoky Pork Chili	114
Sour Cream Cheesecake	77
Sour Cream Pork Chops	107
Southern Beef Pot Roast	126
Soy Braised Chicken	41
Spanish Chorizo Dip	19
Spiced Buffalo Wings	18
Spiced Butter Chicken	39
Spiced Chicken over Wild Rice	39
Spiced Coffee	96
Spiced Creamy Pumpkin Soup	60
Spiced Lemon Cider Punch	97
Spiced Plum Pork Chops	112
Spiced Poached Pears	75
Spiced Pork Belly	116
Spiced Pumpkin Toddy	94
Spiced Rice Pudding	75
Spiced White Chocolate	91
Spicy Asian-Style Mushrooms	27
Spicy Black Bean Soup	55
Spicy Chili Soup with Tomatillos	65
Spicy Enchilada Dip	27
Spicy Glazed Pecans	28
Spicy Hot Chicken Thighs	46
Spicy Monterey Jack Fondue	31
Spicy Mulled Red Wine	99

Split Pea Sausage Soup	55
Sriracha Style Corned Beef	134
Sticky Glazed Pork Ribs	120
Strawberry Fudgy Brownies	71
Sweet and Sour Pork Chops	111
Sweet and Tangy Short Ribs	127
Sweet Corn Chowder	56
Sweet Corn Crab Dip	21
Sweet Corn Jalapeño Dip	30
Sweet Glazed Chicken Drumsticks	44
Sweet Potato Pork Stew	109
Swiss Cheese Fondue	29
Swiss Cheese Saucy Chicken	47
Szechuan Roasted Pork	119

T

Taco Dip	29
Tahini Cheese Dip	31
Tahini Chickpea Dip	32
Tangy Italian Shredded Beef	126
Tarragon Chicken	47
Teriyaki Chicken Wings	33
Teriyaki Pork Tenderloin	106
Texas-Style Braised Beef	130
Thai Chicken Vegetable Medley	45
The Ultimate Hot Chocolate	100
Three Bean Soup	52
Three Cheese Artichoke Sauce	27
Three Pepper Roasted Pork Tenderloin	123
Thyme-Flavored White Bean Pork Cassoulet	115
Tiramisu Bread Pudding	75
Tomato Beef Soup	53
Tomato Beef Stew	129
Tomato Sauce Pork Roast	111
Tomato Soy Glazed Chicken	43
Tropical Meatballs	18
Turmeric Chicken Stew	40
Tuscan Chicken Soup	53

Made in the USA
Las Vegas, NV
10 November 2024